Exclusive Online Resources for You

As our valued reader, your purchase of this book includes access to exclusive online resources designed to enhance your learning experience. These resources can be downloaded from our website, www.vibrantpublishers. com, and are created to help you apply essential advertising concepts effectively.

Online resources for this book include the following essential templates:

1. Brand Consistency Checklist
2. Brand DNA Worksheet
3. Call to Action Builder Guide
4. Color Chart
5. Content Creation Plan Exercise
6. Cultural Sensitivity Checklist
7. Developing Your Advertising Strategy
8. Emotional Trigger Map
9. Engagement Checklist
10. Ethical Advertising Checklist
11. Influencer Marketing Worksheet
12. Persuasion - Manipulation Guide
13. Platform Content Creation Plan
14. SWOT Analysis Template
15. The Ultimate Headline Writing Cheatsheet

I0028028

Why are these online resources valuable?

- **Practical application:** These hands-on tools help you directly apply key advertising concepts to real-world campaigns.
- **Strategic clarity:** Each resource guides you in building focused, ethical, and results-driven advertising strategies.
- **Creative confidence:** From headlines to brand voice, you gain the structure and inspiration to craft standout content with consistency.

How to access your online resources:

1. **Visit the website:** Go to www.vibrantpublishers.com
2. **Find your book:** Navigate to the book's product page via the "Shop" menu or by searching for the book title in the search bar.
3. **Request the resources:** Scroll down to the "Request Sample Book/ Online Resource" section.
4. **Enter your details:** Enter your preferred email ID and select "Online Resource" as the resource type. Lastly, select "user type" and submit the request.
5. **Check your inbox:** The resources will be delivered directly to your email.

Alternatively, for quick access: simply scan the QR code below to go directly to the product page and request the online resources by filling in the required details.

bit.ly/ma-slm

Happy learning!

SELF-LEARNING MANAGEMENT SERIES

VIBRANT
PUBLISHERS

MODERN
ADVERTISING
ESSENTIALS

YOU ALWAYS WANTED TO KNOW

The advertising playbook for brands
that refuse to be ignored

MARIA ISA

MODERN ADVERTISING ESSENTIALS YOU ALWAYS WANTED TO KNOW

First Edition

Published by Vibrant Publishers LLC, USA, www.vibrantpublishers.com

Paperback ISBN 13: 978-1-63651-485-7
Ebook ISBN 13: 978-1-63651-486-4
Hardback ISBN 13: 978-1-63651-487-1

Library of Congress Control Number: 2025935454

This publication is designed to provide accurate and authoritative information in regard to the subject matter covered. The Author has made every effort in the preparation of this book to ensure the accuracy of the information. However, information in this book is sold without warranty either expressed or implied. The Author or the Publisher will not be liable for any damages caused or alleged to be caused either directly or indirectly by this book.

All trademarks and registered trademarks mentioned in this publication are the property of their respective owners. These trademarks are used for editorial and educational purposes only, without intent to infringe upon any trademark rights. This publication is independent and has not been authorized, endorsed, or approved by any trademark owner.

Vibrant Publishers' books are available at special quantity discount for sales promotions, or for use in corporate training programs. For more information please write to bulkorders@vibrantpublishers.com

Please email feedback / corrections (technical, grammatical or spelling) to spellerrors@vibrantpublishers.com

Vibrant publishes in a variety of print and electronic formats and by print-on-demand. Some material included with standard print versions of this book may not be included in e-books or in print-on-demand. To access the complete catalogue of Vibrant Publishers, visit www.vibrantpublishers.com

SELF-LEARNING MANAGEMENT SERIES

TITLE	PAPERBACK* ISBN

BUSINESS AND ENTREPRENEURSHIP

TITLE	PAPERBACK* ISBN
BUSINESS COMMUNICATION ESSENTIALS	9781636511634
BUSINESS ETHICS ESSENTIALS	9781636513324
BUSINESS LAW ESSENTIALS	9781636511702
BUSINESS PLAN ESSENTIALS	9781636511214
BUSINESS STRATEGY ESSENTIALS	9781949395778
ENTREPRENEURSHIP ESSENTIALS	9781636511603
INTERNATIONAL BUSINESS ESSENTIALS	9781636513294
PRINCIPLES OF MANAGEMENT ESSENTIALS	9781636511542

COMPUTER SCIENCE AND TECHNOLOGY

TITLE	PAPERBACK* ISBN
BLOCKCHAIN ESSENTIALS	9781636513003
MACHINE LEARNING ESSENTIALS	9781636513775
PYTHON ESSENTIALS	9781636512938

DATA SCIENCE FOR BUSINESS

TITLE	PAPERBACK* ISBN
BUSINESS INTELLIGENCE ESSENTIALS	9781636513362
DATA ANALYTICS ESSENTIALS	9781636511184

FINANCIAL LITERACY AND ECONOMICS

TITLE	PAPERBACK* ISBN
COST ACCOUNTING & MANAGEMENT ESSENTIALS	9781636511030
FINANCIAL ACCOUNTING ESSENTIALS	9781636510972
FINANCIAL MANAGEMENT ESSENTIALS	9781636511009
MACROECONOMICS ESSENTIALS	9781636511818
MICROECONOMICS ESSENTIALS	9781636511153
PERSONAL FINANCE ESSENTIALS	9781636511849
PRINCIPLES OF ECONOMICS ESSENTIALS	9781636512334

*Also available in Hardback & Ebook formats

SELF-LEARNING MANAGEMENT SERIES

TITLE	PAPERBACK* ISBN

HR, DIVERSITY, AND ORGANIZATIONAL SUCCESS

DIVERSITY, EQUITY, AND INCLUSION ESSENTIALS	9781636512976
DIVERSITY IN THE WORKPLACE ESSENTIALS	9781636511122
HR ANALYTICS ESSENTIALS	9781636510347
HUMAN RESOURCE MANAGEMENT ESSENTIALS	9781949395839
ORGANIZATIONAL BEHAVIOR ESSENTIALS	9781636512303
ORGANIZATIONAL DEVELOPMENT ESSENTIALS	9781636511481

LEADERSHIP AND PERSONAL DEVELOPMENT

DECISION MAKING ESSENTIALS	9781636510026
INDIA'S ROAD TO TRANSFORMATION: WHY LEADERSHIP MATTERS	9781636512273
LEADERSHIP ESSENTIALS	9781636510316
TIME MANAGEMENT ESSENTIALS	9781636511665

MODERN MARKETING AND SALES

CONSUMER BEHAVIOR ESSENTIALS	9781636513263
DIGITAL MARKETING ESSENTIALS	9781949395747
MARKETING MANAGEMENT ESSENTIALS	9781636511788
MARKET RESEARCH ESSENTIALS	9781636513744
SALES MANAGEMENT ESSENTIALS	9781636510743
SERVICES MARKETING ESSENTIALS	9781636511733
SOCIAL MEDIA MARKETING ESSENTIALS	9781636512181

*Also available in Hardback & Ebook formats

SELF-LEARNING MANAGEMENT SERIES

TITLE	PAPERBACK* ISBN

OPERATIONS MANAGEMENT

AGILE ESSENTIALS	9781636510057
OPERATIONS & SUPPLY CHAIN MANAGEMENT ESSENTIALS	9781949395242
PROJECT MANAGEMENT ESSENTIALS	9781636510712
STAKEHOLDER ENGAGEMENT ESSENTIALS	9781636511511

CURRENT AFFAIRS

DIGITAL SHOCK	9781636513805

*Also available in Hardback & Ebook formats

About the Author

Maria Isa has a rare talent for understanding brands. As a results-driven marketing strategist for some of the world's most recognized companies, such as Unilever, Nestlé, Colgate-Palmolive, and Mondelēz, she has contributed to campaigns that have had an impact on how millions interact with household names.

Ever-curious about the subtle science behind what makes brands thrive, Maria has spent her career building a keen awareness of how brands build loyal communities.

Her expertise is practical and deeply informed, drawing from her marketing and management education at the University of Witwatersrand in South Africa. She is a passionate doer of things and recently authored "How to Build a Bankable Brand" to educate non-marketers on the business of branding.

Maria now lives in Dar es Salaam, Tanzania, where she consults local and international companies on how best to navigate a changing marketing landscape. She believes that successful brands prioritize connection to stay ahead of the competition.

As you turn the pages of this book, you'll gain insider insights into advertising strategies that merge psychology, strategy, and commercial success. Maria offers more than techniques; she shares a way of thinking that transforms advertising from an expense into an investment.

What Experts Say About This Book!

This book is like holding the entire advertising industry in your hands.

– Pete Barry, Author,
Advertising Concept Book 3E: Think Now, Design Later

This is a fantastic book for anyone wanting to learn about how advertising works. It's written in an easy-to-understand manner and sets out at the start that the reader should only dip into the parts that are required. It's an incredibly useful reference resource that I will come back to time and time again.

– Ian J Cole, YouTuber

As an advertising professor, I've been waiting for a book like this one. I often feel like I have to convince students to read the textbook, but not with *Modern Advertising Essentials You Always Wanted to Know*. It begins with an engaging history of advertising that pulled me in with nostalgic examples and the energy of digital media. I especially appreciated how it introduces social psychology as the foundation of advertising, which mirrors how I teach both digital marketing and advertising.

Each chapter builds on the last to create a strong, practical framework. By the end, readers know exactly how to apply key strategies and tools with confidence. While many advertising books lean too heavily on theory or trends, Maria Isa's guide focuses on what truly matters. It is grounded in consumer behavior, full of real-world case studies, and written with both students and professionals in mind. I'll be adopting it in my own course.

– Lisa Power, Associate Professor of Marketing,
Saint Martin's University

Table of Contents

Preface

Why do some brands capture hearts and loyalty whilst others struggle to stand out? Moreover, how can you, as a business owner, marketer, or creative professional, use advertising to form genuine connections with your audience that drive sales?

I've written this book to bust some myths about advertising and show how it works in real life. It's not necessarily about flashy billboards or funny slogans. Advertising is a well-thought-through mix of psychology, storytelling, data, and technology. The aim is for you to understand how all these aspects work together, avoid being overlooked, and produce adverts that drive engagement, conversation, and action.

We live in an age where consumer behavior is evolving faster than ever. The frequent emergence of new technologies, social media platforms, and shifting cultural trends mean that what worked last year is almost past its best-before date today. This book is designed to help you stay ahead. Whether you're a business owner attempting to make sense of online advertising, a business in need of fine-tuning your marketing approach, or a student looking to grasp the subtleties of influencer persuasion, this book will equip you with the ability to craft advertising that sells.

Unlike traditional, beginner-level books that dwell on dry theories, this book is structured to be practical, engaging, and actionable. You'll find:

- Real-world case studies that break down successful campaigns and the strategies behind them
- Insights from consumer psychology to help you understand why people buy

- Step-by-step frameworks to create compelling, high-converting ads
- Ethical considerations to ensure your advertising builds trust rather than exploits
- Forward-looking perspectives on what advertising is becoming in the Artificial Intelligence (AI), automation, and immersive world

If you're hoping to learn how to manipulate your consumer to drive sales, this book is not for you. If you're here to figure out how to make advertising work for you while building value for end-users and communities, continue reading.

Introduction to the Book

Think about the last thing you purchased. Was it a meal, some gadget, or a fresh set of sneakers? Now, ask yourself: *What led you to that purchase?* Was it an Instagram ad that caught your eye? A YouTube review? A discount email that landed at just the right time?

Advertising is everywhere, telling us what to spend our money on, what to think, and what we should aspire to. Advertisers can make a difference, inspire, and unite, but with the saturation of cyberspace today, it takes more than just sleek graphics and memorable slogans to stand out from the crowd.

This book is about understanding the science and psychology behind effective advertising. It's about becoming a master storyteller, captivating your audience, and taking them on a journey to their dream destination (that conveniently coincides with your bank address). Let's be real: advertising is still a business.

Why read this book?

Successful advertising delivers results that matter to stakeholders, like visibility, profits, and social impact. However, most advertising books focus on one aspect only: either the art of persuasion (storytelling, branding, and emotional appeal) or the science of performance (analytics, targeting, and data-driven decision-making).

Consider this book your field manual for modern advertising because:

- It blends creativity and strategy. You'll learn not only how to craft compelling ads but also how to analyze and refine them based on performance data.
- It's practical and real-world focused. Every concept is backed by case studies, industry insights, and proven frameworks you can apply immediately.
- It's built for today's fast-changing landscape. From social media to AI-driven advertising, it covers what works *right now*.

The goal of this book is simple: to turn you into a skilled advertiser who can create ads that get attention, build trust, and drive action.

What you'll gain from this book

When you're finished reading, you'll be able to:

- Understand why people buy and how to craft messages that speak to their emotions.
- Master digital and traditional advertising, from TV and billboards to TikTok and YouTube ads.
- Dissect successful ad campaigns and apply their strategies to your projects.
- Use psychology-based persuasion techniques to supercharge engagement and conversions.
- Track ad performance and make data-driven decisions to deliver more of the results you want.
- Stay ahead of new trends in AI, personalization, and experiential ads.

Spoiler alert

I've taken the best insights from psychology, branding, and digital marketing and distilled them into a straightforward, actionable guide. Here's a sneak peek at how I've structured each chapter for you to get the most out of these pages:

- Clear, actionable insights that simplify complex advertising concepts
- Breakdowns of real-world campaigns to see what works (and what doesn't)
- Proven strategies to craft high-performing ads across different platforms
- Interactive exercises that reinforce key lessons and sharpen your skills

Acknowledgments

I want to sincerely thank God for this opportunity to pass on my knowledge and share my passion with fellow marketers and advertising enthusiasts.

Thank you to my younger sister, Neema Isa, for her continued support and guidance.

Who Can Benefit From This Book?

The truth is that advertising is for anyone who wants to spread an idea, build a brand, or persuade an audience. With that in mind, the table below provides an outline of how this book can help specific readers in their unique situations. Based on the specific type of reader and the need, one can get a glimpse of what awaits them on these pages.

Type of reader	The need	How this book can help
Entrepreneurs and business owners	To stop wasting money on ads that don't convert	Maximize every ad dollar and create campaigns that convert.
Marketing and advertising professionals	To stay ahead of evolving trends	Master data-backed strategies and psychology-driven messaging that modern consumers respond to.
Students and aspiring advertisers	To break free from theory-heavy learning	Get hands-on strategies that agencies and brands are using today so you graduate with real-world skills.
Freelancers and content creators	To get traction with your ads	Master the fundamentals of high-performing ads.
Curious about advertising	To understand how advertising works and why you're constantly seeing the same ads	Understand how brands influence behavior.
Corporate teams and in-house marketers	To align ad strategies with business goals	Develop brand-consistent campaigns, refine targeting, and ensure measurable success.
Nonprofits and social causes	To spread a message, not sell a product	Create persuasive campaigns that drive impact where it's most needed.

How to Use This Book?

This is a practical, actionable, and adaptable book. You don't need to read it from cover to cover in one sitting. Feel free to jump to the parts that apply to you, understand the strategies that work, and implement them accordingly.

Getting the most value from this read is as simple as counting to four:

1. **Start where you need it most**

   Whether you're creating ad copy, optimizing targeting strategy, or analyzing campaign performance, go straight to the section that helps you solve your immediate challenge. This book is structured for quick access and real-world application—use it however it suits you.

2. **Learn the strategy, see it in action**

   The book focuses on practical insights you can implement right away. Every concept is backed up by real-life examples. You'll see what works, what lessons others have learned the hard way, and why.

3. **Apply the strategies**

   Knowing something and using it are two different things. That's why this book is designed for execution. You'll find:

   - Step-by-step frameworks to guide your campaigns
   - Exercises and prompts to sharpen your advertising instincts.
   - Checklists to keep your ads on track

4. Stay future-ready

The advertising world never stands still, and neither should you. Use this book to understand today's landscape while staying agile enough to adapt to what's next. The best advertisers never stop learning. Continue to refine, experiment, and evolve.

CHAPTER 1

From Billboards to Bytes: The Evolution of Advertising

Key Learning Objectives

- How newspapers, radio, and billboards laid the foundation for modern advertising.
- Why TV transformed advertising with stories, jingles, and iconic slogans.
- How the internet turned advertising into a data-driven, interactive experience.
- The role of social media in creating two-way conversations between brands and consumers.
- How viral campaigns and influencer marketing changed the way brands connect with audiences.

Advertising is a tool used to raise brand awareness. Media platforms that advertising relied on in the past have changed as a result of changing consumption patterns by consumers. Newspaper ads, basic radio, and television were the first media to be used, and then social media and viral campaigns emerged with the digital age. The history of advertising and how each era influenced the commercials we see now will be covered in this chapter.

As we go through the turning points in advertising history, you will see that it is more than creativity; it's also about timing, strategy, and psychology. By the conclusion of this chapter, you will gain a clearer understanding of how the world has been affected and influenced by advertising. You will discover why it remains one of the most intriguing and important industries globally today.

1.1 Old School Advertising: Newspapers, Radio, and Billboards

1.1.1 Newspapers

In the early days, newspapers were the gold standard for spreading the word. They offered advertisers a unique opportunity to reach specific audiences based on distribution areas. Long advertisements were jam-packed with text explaining why a product was worthwhile or why a particular event was worth going to.

One of the first companies to use print advertising was Procter & Gamble, which displayed straightforward but effective advertisements for goods like candles and soap. Their strategy established the standard for brands to hold themselves to.

David Ogilvy, famously known as the "Father of Advertising," championed this era with his belief: *"The more you tell, the more you sell."* His endorsement of detailed ads helped shape the narrative style of early print media.

1.1.2 Radio

Radio transformed advertising in the early 20th century by adding voice, emotion, and immediacy to marketing messages. Families would gather around their radios each evening, creating a captive audience for advertisers to reach directly. Sponsorship quickly became a go-to strategy, with brands funding popular programs and seamlessly inserting their messages into the content.

For example, Camel Cigarettes famously sponsored news broadcasts and repeated the memorable slogan, "More doctors smoke Camels," aligning their product with the trust and authority of the medical profession. This strategic repetition, promoted by advertising pioneer Rosser Reeves, who was known for saying, "You have to make the customer remember you," helped make brands unforgettable by embedding them in listeners' daily routines. Radio jingles and slogans, often catchy and relatable, reinforced this effect, turning ads into cultural staples. The enduring principles of authority, trust, and repetition continue to shape advertising today.

1.1.3 Billboards

The early 20th century saw the rise of billboards as a mainstay of outdoor advertising. Billboards were placed in urban areas and along busy roadways. Their goal? Deliver a punchy and memorable message in a matter of seconds. To deliver on this, bold visuals and minimal text became their trademark.

| Figure 1.1 | "GOT MILK?" BILLBOARD CAMPAIGN |

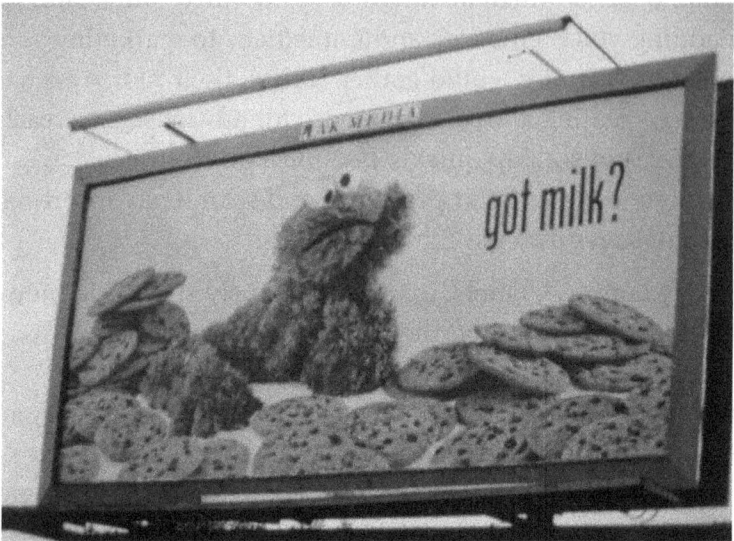

Source: (Miller, 2014)

One prime example of effective billboard advertising is the "Got Milk?" campaign illustrated in Figure 1.1. It was memorable due to its simplicity: a powerful visual combined with an easy-to-remember tagline. These billboards proved that in advertising, less is more, which was in sharp contrast to the earlier approaches used in newspapers.

Why Billboards Worked

High Visibility: It was impossible to overlook billboards, particularly in places with plenty of traffic.

Memorable Messaging: Viewers retained clear, succinct messages long after they had passed.

Mass Appeal: They effectively reached a variety of audiences by reaching commuters, drivers, and walkers.

1.2 TV Takes Over

When TVs became household items in the 50s and 60s, advertising entered its golden era. TV had sight, sound, and motion, so brands could tell stories in 30 seconds. Advertisers could emotionally connect with viewers by showing their products in action on TV. Leading the way were companies like Procter & Gamble, who created "soap operas" or TV shows supported by companies that sell cleaning products and cleverly wove commercials into their storylines. This worked well because soap operas blurred the line between entertainment and advertising, subtly nudging viewers to buy the products being featured.

Combining sight, sound, and motion, television gave advertising a new dimension. Its employment of jingles and slogans is arguably one of its most enduring accomplishments. These musical hooks turned into cultural phenomena that ingrained themselves into generations' worth of collective memory. Beyond the actual goods, a memorable phrase or catchy melody could evoke strong emotions, encourage brand loyalty, and even influence societal norms. Due to its immense popularity, the re-recorded version of the song "I'd Like to Teach the World to Sing" became a global hit. It is still considered one of the most memorable moments in advertising history, even after decades have passed.

Coca-Cola's ad, "I'd Like to Buy the World a Coke", which first aired in 1971, showcased a cross-section of young people singing for peace and harmony to the music of an older jingle named "True Love and Apple Pie." You can find a link to this video on the online resource page.

It was more than an ad for a drink. Besides peddling a drink, this ad peddled peace and love. An unassuming yet powerful message. Coca-Cola then became a symbol of solidarity by linking these feelings to its beverage.

1.2.1 Slogans

As succinct verbal descriptions of a brand's identity or value proposition, slogans frequently complement jingles. Because it captures a brand's essence in a few words, a brilliant slogan resonates.

Examples of Iconic Slogans include:

- Nike's "Just Do It" which serves as a motivational call to action that is not limited to sports.
- KitKat's *"Gimmie a break, Gimmie a break, break me off a piece of that KitKat Bar,"* which encourages taking a moment to pause during life's busy moments.
- L'Oréal's "Because You're Worth It," which provides a positive affirmation of the target audience's value.

1.2.2 Jingles

Even if they haven't been as popular lately, traditional jingles continue to be used in contemporary advertising campaigns. By developing sound logos or musical cues that accomplish the same goal, brands have responded to digital platforms and consumers' shorter attention spans. For example, a brief sound effect known as "Tudum" is used by Netflix to announce the beginning of content, eliciting a Pavlovian reaction from viewers.

Because jingles appeal directly to the emotional and memory centers of the brain, their combination with slogans is incredibly powerful. Here's how the science behind it works:

- **Repetition Builds Memory:** Neural pathways in the brain are strengthened by repetition, imprinting the tune into long-term memory. People can still hum it with ease many years later, proving that repetition helps a message stick in people's minds.

> **! Note**
>
> Music activates the brain's limbic system, which governs emotions and memory. When paired with a product, a jingle strengthens the emotional bond and leaves a lasting imprint in the audience's mind.

- **Music and Feeling:** From joy to moving memories, music has a unique ability to create strong emotional connections. A jingle that embodies the brand's joyful and positive spirit can evolve into more than just a promotional catchphrase but a cultural symbol of joy and satisfaction.

See examples of these on the online resources page

The most memorable slogans and jingles are frequently the most straightforward. They employ brief melodies or phrases that are simple to recall and mimic. Jingles and slogans guarantee that their message is strongly ingrained in audiences by establishing an emotional connection with them. Successful campaigns seem relevant and personal because they represent the beliefs and goals of their target audience.

Jingles and slogans are cultural symbols that are more than merely advertising tools. They preserve the essence of their time through the establishment in the minds of the public. The combination of sounds and catchphrases has proven to influence customer behavior, increase sales, and create emotional bonds. The same principles that allowed advertising to thrive in the past still apply today.

1.3 Digital Disruption: How the Internet Changed Everything

The internet transformed the advertising landscape by offering brands an interactive, data-informed way to engage and connect with consumers. Conventional media, such as newspapers and television, provided extensive coverage but lacked feedback on their effectiveness. The internet transformed advertising into a science, providing valuable insights from every click, impression, and conversion. This enabled advertisers to modify campaigns instantly and create experiences that truly connected with each individual.

The initial banner ad was made by AT&T in 1994 and represented a straightforward yet groundbreaking advancement. This advertisement transcended mere engagement. It posed the question: Is it possible for advertising to be interactive?

Figure 1.2 **AT&T BANNER AD 1994**

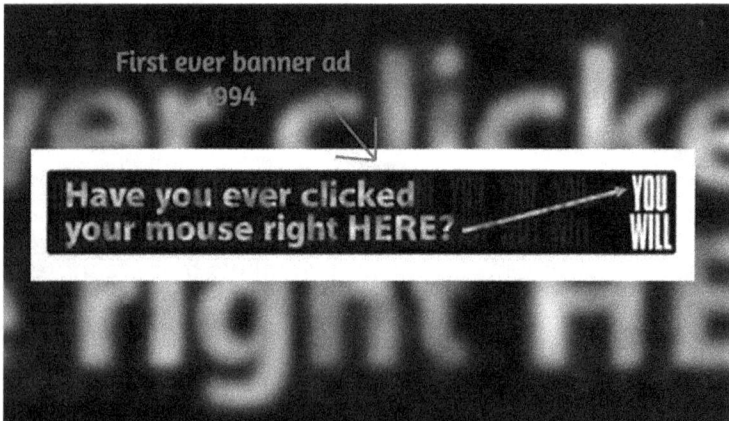

Source: (Mediashotz, 2024)

The first banner ad, which simply said, "Click Here," had a 44% click-through rate, which is far lower than the norm for today, but it was surprisingly successful. It marked the beginning of an era where advertisers could track user behavior in real time.

Google AdWords took it even further. By looking at user data like search history, location, and browsing habits, brands could deliver super-targeted ads. For example, a search for "best running shoes" might trigger a Nike ad showing off their latest designs. The seamless connection between consumer intent and brand presence made advertising more relevant than ever, with less waste and more engagement.

Just as big was the internet's ability to make advertising shareable. Viral campaigns became the hallmark of the digital age, turning audiences into collaborators who amplified brand messages through likes, shares, and retweets. Old Spice's "The Man Your Man Could Smell Like" campaign used humor and relatability to go global. Oreo's tweet during the 2013 Super Bowl blackout was another all-time great: "You can still dunk in the dark."

Figure 1.3 OREO TWEET DURING 2013 SUPERBOWL BLACKOUT

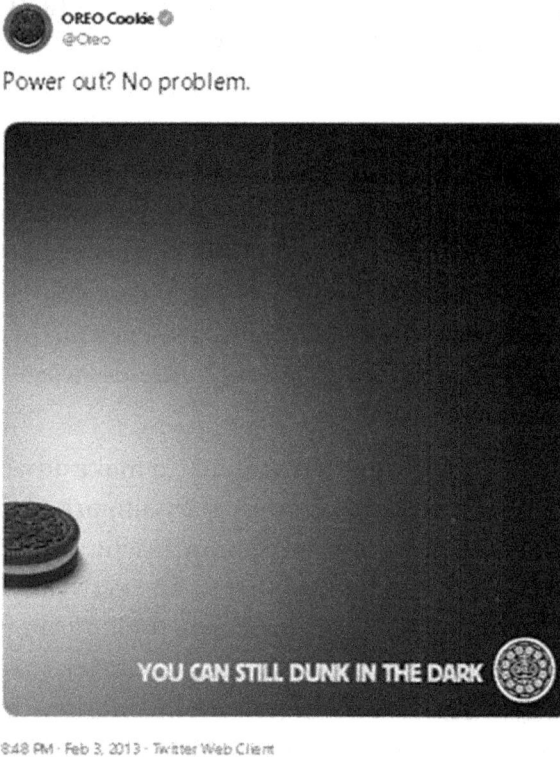

OREO Cookie
@Oreo

Power out? No problem.

YOU CAN STILL DUNK IN THE DARK

8:48 PM · Feb 3, 2013 · Twitter Web Client

Source: (OREO, 2013)

During the 2013 Super Bowl blackout, Oreo famously tweeted, "You can still dunk in the dark." Published just moments after the power outage, the tweet garnered over 15,000 retweets and earned acclaim for its real-time relevance and cleverness.

Figure 1.4 illustrates the progression from AT&T's first banner ad to the company's current AI-powered, interactive marketing initiatives, demonstrating how advancements in technology and targeting have expanded the possibilities of digital advertising.

Figure 1.4   HOW DIGITAL ADVERTISING DEVELOPED

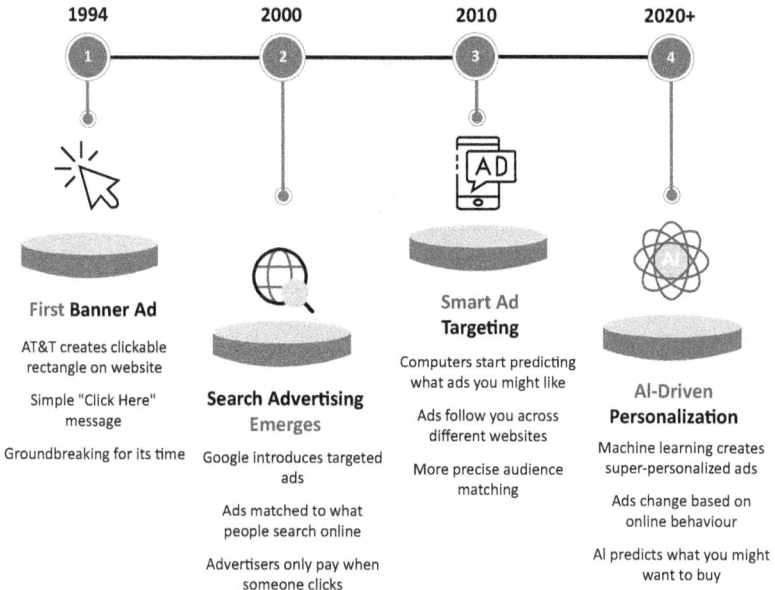

1994	2000	2010	2020+
1	**2**	**3**	**4**

First Banner Ad

AT&T creates clickable rectangle on website

Simple "Click Here" message

Groundbreaking for its time

Search Advertising Emerges

Google introduces targeted ads

Ads matched to what people search online

Advertisers only pay when someone clicks

Smart Ad Targeting

Computers start predicting what ads you might like

Ads follow you across different websites

More precise audience matching

AI-Driven Personalization

Machine learning creates super-personalized ads

Ads change based on online behaviour

AI predicts what you might want to buy

1.4 Social Media and Influencers: The Latest Standard

Social media changed advertising from a one-way communication into an interactive conversation, allowing consumers to reply, share, and participate in content creation. Its key advantage is its capacity to target specific audiences precisely. Algorithms examine users' preferences, activities, and characteristics to present advertisements that seem appropriate and timely.

For instance, a cosmetics company like Sephora can aim at users who follow makeup content creators or regularly interact with tutorials. This degree of customization guarantees that advertisements are both impactful and significant.

Table 1.1	AVERAGE ACTIVE SOCIAL NETWORK USERS PER MONTH

Social Network	Monthly active users
Facebook	3.07 billion
YouTube	2.5 billion
Instagram	2 billion
WhatsApp	2 billion
TikTok	1.09 billion

Source: (KEPIOS,2024)

As shown in Table 1.1, which shows the number of users by social media platform, these platforms offer brands unique opportunities to showcase their personalities, engage in creative consumer interactions, and use user-generated content to reach a larger audience.

Over time, social media introduces new tools to boost engagement, such as polls, challenges, and interactive stories. TikTok, for instance, excels at turning user-generated content into viral campaigns.

Ocean Spray's surprising triumph on the platform started with a straightforward, genuine video: someone skateboarding while drinking cranberry juice and enjoying Fleetwood Mac's "Dreams." The video resonated with audiences, generating a surge of related posts and increasing Ocean Spray's brand awareness. The video resonated with audiences, igniting a surge of related posts and enhancing Ocean Spray's brand awareness. The company took advantage of the phenomenon by delivering a significant shipment of its products to the creator, further boosting its visibility. Watch this video through the link provided on our online resources page.

Wendy's activity on Twitter serves as another example of how social media allows brands to connect with audiences in creative and inventive ways. Celebrated for its witty and often daring posts, Wendy's built a reputation on authenticity and humor.

A notable moment came when they roasted McDonald's with the tweet, "Your beef is frozen, and we'd like to remind you we're not talking about the Twitter kind." These interactions not only entertained audiences but also reinforced Wendy's brand identity as approachable, bold, and culturally relevant.

Figure 1.5   WENDY TO MCDONALD'S VIA TWITTER

McDonald's ✓
@McDonalds

Today we've announced that by mid-2018, all Quarter Pounder burgers at the majority of our restaurants will be cooked with fresh beef.

1:16 PM - Mar 30, 2017

💬 1,241   🔁 5,893   ♡ 8,051

Wendy's ✓
@Wendys

Replying to @McDonalds

.@McDonalds So you'll still use frozen beef in MOST of your burgers in ALL of your restaurants? Asking for a friend.

4:00 PM - Mar 30, 2017

💬 7,672   🔁 73,582   ♡ 182,087

Source: (WENDY'S, 2017)

Wendy's answers are spot-on, in addition to being humorous. Wendy's has turned its X (formerly known as Twitter) account into a global phenomenon by projecting an image of a cheeky, confident, and personable individual.

A transformative aspect of social media is influencer marketing. In contrast to conventional celebrity endorsements, influencers foster trust and relatability with their audience, causing their suggestions to appear more authentic and personal. Daniel Wellington's ascent to international fame highlights the effectiveness of this approach.

By partnering with influencers who shared aspirational yet accessible content featuring their watches, the brand turned its timepieces into a lifestyle symbol. Figure 1.6 illustrates the factors that drive virality, such as emotional resonance, shareability, relatability, and entertainment value.

Figure 1.6 | KEY DRIVERS OF VIRALITY

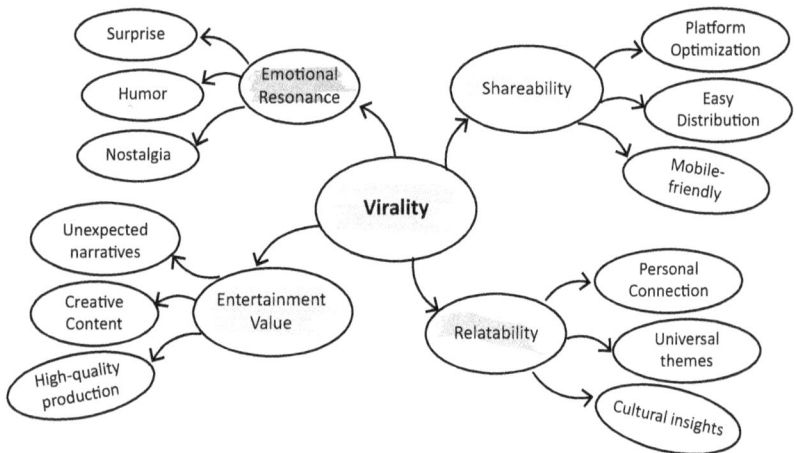

Chapter Summary

- The first important advertising medium was newspapers, which used complex messaging to influence and educate readers.

- Radio introduced voices and jingles, which made commercials unique and memorable.

- Through the use of sound, vision, and motion, television transformed advertisements into emotionally engaging stories.

- Through interaction and accurate targeting, the internet revolutionized advertising by enabling brands to engage more effectively with specific audiences.

- Social media encouraged in-person interactions with customers, turning advertising into a conversation.

- Viral campaigns show how creative thinking, combined with a strong emotional bond, can turn ordinary ideas into worldwide phenomena.

- Instagram and TikTok represent two platforms that enable brands to interact with consumers (through challenges, hashtags, and various interactive elements).

- Finding inventive methods to engage consumers has always been the goal of advertising; however, the tools utilized may change. The fundamental objective, however, remains unchanged: engaging the audience. This is crucial because it ensures that brands can maintain their relevance in an ever-evolving market. Although the approach may differ, the essence of connection persists.

Quiz

1. **What was one of the earliest ways advertisers reached large audiences?**
   a. Social media
   b. Television
   c. Newspapers
   d. Influencer marketing

2. **Why was radio such an exciting platform for advertisers?**
   a. It allowed brands to use music, voices, and jingles to make their ads feel personal.
   b. It combined sight, sound, and motion.
   c. It relied on data-driven targeting.
   d. It was the first interactive advertising platform.

3. **What made television ads so powerful?**
   a. They used real-time analytics to track viewers.
   b. They told stories, featured jingles, and emotionally connected with audiences.
   c. They depended on social media to spread their message.
   d. They were mostly text-based and informative.

4. **Which campaign is an example of successful viral marketing?**
   a. Coca-Cola's "Share a Coke"
   b. Marlboro's "Marlboro Man"
   c. McDonald's "I'm Lovin' It"
   d. Nationwide's "On Your Side"

5. **Why are influencers so effective in advertising today?**
   a. They create ads that feel personal and relatable to their audiences.
   b. They use long, detailed messaging like early newspaper ads.
   c. They focus only on billboards and TV.
   d. They rely on jingles and slogans to appeal to everyone.

6. **What makes a campaign go viral?**
   a. It has detailed explanations about the product.
   b. It evokes strong emotions, is relatable, and is easy to share.
   c. It focuses on radio and newspaper advertising.
   d. It relies only on celebrity endorsements.

7. **What was the purpose of jingles in early TV advertising?**
   a. To provide long-form educational content
   b. To evoke emotions and make ads more memorable
   c. To replace visuals entirely
   d. To promote competition between brands

8. **How did radio advertising leverage trust?**
   a. By providing interactive ad formats
   b. By sponsoring trusted programs and using authoritative slogans
   c. By offering discounts in ads
   d. By focusing on visual storytelling

9. Who is known as the "Father of Advertising"?
   a. Rosser Reeves
   b. Philip Kotler
   c. Seth Godin
   d. David Ogilvy

10. Which phrase summarizes the value of a memorable slogan?
    a. "It guarantees sales."
    b. "It simplifies ad production."
    c. "It encapsulates a brand's identity in just a few words."
    d. "It eliminates the need for visuals."

Answers

1 – c	2 – a	3 – b	4 – a	5 – a
6 – b	7 – b	8 – b	9 – d	10 – c

Case Study: Coca-Cola Campaign: "Share a Coke"

This campaign showcased how, when executed effectively and with attention to consumer tastes, a straightforward concept can revitalize a globally recognized brand. In 2011, it was initially launched in Australia, substituting the Coca-Cola logo on bottles with 150 of the nation's most famous names. What began as a minor trial transformed into a worldwide sensation that boosted sales, interaction, and customer loyalty.

The Idea

The idea was straightforward but bold: putting consumers' names on Coca-Cola bottles to encourage a sense of ownership and personal connection. It changed how the Coca-Cola logo, which is among the most recognizable in the world, was traditionally applied in a strict and regulated manner. Customers responded to personalization on a human level, turning a mass-produced good into a unique and contagious experience.

Coca-Cola tested the idea for the first time in Australia by secretly distributing bottles with 150 popular names on them. Customers started sharing pictures of the customized bottles on social media as soon as they saw them. People were excited to see their name on a Coke bottle, leading to a phenomenon despite there being no official launch for the campaign.

A couple of weeks later, Coca-Cola launched the campaign and encouraged people to post pictures of their custom bottles on Facebook and Instagram. A global phenomenon arose from the hashtag #ShareaCoke.

Coca-Cola rolled out the campaign in over 70 countries, adapting to local languages and customs to build on the success. In some markets, they used nicknames and phrases instead of names. For example, in China, they used "bestie" and "classmate" on the bottles as they usually use both names and a lot of people have the same name.

Watch the commercial through the link provided on the online resources page.

Sales and Engagement

The "Share a Coke" campaign reversed a decade of declining sales in key markets:

- In Australia, Coca-Cola saw a 7% increase in consumption among young adults.
- In the US, sales were up 2%, a big achievement for a mature brand.
- 150 million customized bottles were sold globally, making the campaign a commercial success.

Social Media Impact

Social media was the heartbeat of this campaign, driving engagement and reach.

- #ShareaCoke had over 500,000 posts on Instagram.
- An 870% increase in Facebook traffic in the first 6 months in Australia.
- 76,000 virtual Coke cans were shared online.
- 998 million Twitter impressions globally.

Why it worked

- **Personalization at Scale:** Large-scale personalization creates a sense of community and connection. Coca-Cola turned its drink into a social currency and conversation starter by putting names on the bottles.

- **Emotional Engagement:** The marketing played on the joy of celebrating and sharing connections. Because of this emotional bond, people shared pictures, shared stories, and bought more Coke.
- **Social Media:** Turned their customers into brand ambassadors by promoting user-generated content and expanding the campaign without extra cost.
- **Market Flexibility:** Coca-Cola used local names and phrases to make the campaign global by localizing it for each market.

The "Share a Coke" campaign shows how companies can:

- **Take calculated risks:** Putting names instead of the Coca-Cola logo was a big risk that paid off.
- **Leverage social media:** Content was used to expand the reach.
- **Localize for effect:** Even global brands can make their products feel personal.

Source: (STORYBOX, 2024)

Exercise: Ad Evolution Timeline

Make a timeline that illustrates the evolution of advertising. Point out significant turning points and talk about how each one altered how brands interact with consumers.

Further Learning

Links also available in Online Resources:

1. **I'd Like to Buy the World a Coke Commercial - 1971**
   http://bit.ly/4fcor8M

2. **Example of repetition to build memory: Alka-Seltzer Plop Plop, Fizz Fizz (1976)**
   http://bit.ly/4lFJONO

3. **Example of music in advertising: McDonald's "I'm Lovin' It"**
   http://bit.ly/3Urgu5S

4. **Ocean's spray TikTok ad: Nathan Apodaca**
   http://bit.ly/3UernYV

5. **Coca-Cola case study commercial: #ShareaCoke**
   https://bit.ly/414UaCN

CHAPTER **2**

We Buy Because

Key Learning Objectives

- How scarcity creates urgency and influences consumer behavior.
- Why social proof encourages us to follow the crowd.
- How emotional appeal builds deep connections with consumers.
- The importance of authority in establishing trust and credibility.
- How brands like Apple have mastered these principles to drive success.

Why do we choose certain products over others? Is it purely their quality, or is there something deeper at work? Competent marketers understand how to appeal to the feelings, actions, and psychological cues that subtly influence our choices. In order to influence our thoughts, emotions, and behaviors, advertising appeals to these values. It uses our emotions, instincts, and social inclinations to its advantage, frequently without our conscious awareness.

These principles aren't new; they've been shaping human behavior for centuries. From the urgency of limited-edition products to the comfort of following the crowd, these triggers work because they align with how our minds naturally function. Once you understand these strategies, you will see ads entirely differently and be able to use this knowledge to your advantage.

You will understand the importance of psychological elements in effective advertising and how they affect consumer behavior by the end of this chapter. You will also learn why one of the most dynamic and influential industries in the modern world is still advertising.

2.1 The Power of Scarcity

Imagine seeing the message "Only 2 left in stock!" while you are shopping online. Do you click "Add to Cart" more quickly than you intended to? That's the power of scarcity at work. We desire things more when they are scarce. Because of the sense of urgency created by scarcity, we feel as though we might miss out if we do not take immediate action.

2.1.1 Why Does Scarcity Work?

Humans are drawn to rarity because it appeals to our primal instinct. Psychologists call this loss aversion. Given the option, we'd rather avoid losing something than gain something new. When an opportunity seems fleeting, our brains perceive it as more valuable, triggering a desire to act quickly.

Think about Black Friday sales or concert tickets for a big artist. The ticking clock and the "limited stock" alerts that typically come with these create a sense of urgency that pushes us to act because of the fear of missing out (FOMO).

2.1.2 How Advertisers Leverage Scarcity

Ads that use urgency cues can boost sales by 30% more than those that don't. The following are some typical indicators used by marketers to persuade consumers to purchase their goods right away:

1. **Limited-Time Offers:** Expressions that convey urgency, such as "Today Only!" and "Flash Sale," are powerful tools in marketing. A prime example of this strategy creating an annual shopping frenzy is Black Friday sales, where customers rush to grab deals before they're gone.

2. **Exclusive Access:** Limited-edition collections and other products marketed as exclusive provide a sense of privilege to those who can afford them. Luxury brands like Rolex and Hermès capitalize on this exclusivity, presenting limited-edition items that serve as status symbols.

3. **Low Stock Alerts:** Online retailers often display "Only 3 left in stock!" to heighten urgency. Amazon's Lightning Deals, for instance, show real-time progress bars of how much stock is left, pushing users to complete their purchases.

2.1.3 The Emotional Pull of Scarcity

Scarcity evokes strong emotions and influences our economic choices. We experience heightened mental activity when we face the possibility of losing out on an opportunity.

Experiencing anxiety, excitement, and a sense of urgency can cause us to make snap judgments.

No one can dispute the appeal of limited-edition trainers. When Nike releases a highly sought-after shoe, usually with only a few thousand pairs available, fans will wait for hours in line both in-store and online. Owning one of these sneakers feels like gaining entry into an exclusive club. The scarcity creates a competitive atmosphere, intensifying the urge to win, and in this case, "winning" means successfully making a purchase.

Scarcity Principle in Action

A fascinating example of the scarcity principle comes from Booking.com. When searching for a hotel, you've likely seen messages like "Only 2 rooms left!" or "3 people are looking at this property right now." These notifications aren't accidental as they're designed to stoke urgency and make you finalize your booking. By showcasing how scarce a desirable option is, Booking. com ensures you feel the pressure to act before someone else beats you to it.

A classic study by Worchel, Lee, and Adewole in 1975 showed how scarcity impacts the perception of value (Eyal, 2013). Participants rated cookies from a jar as more desirable when the jar contained only two cookies versus ten, even though the cookies were identical. Similar experiments conducted over the years have provided similar results, showing that scarcity makes us value things more when they're harder to get.

Exercise 2.1: Create a Scarcity-Driven Ad

Choose a fictional product, like limited-edition sneakers or exclusive wireless earbuds, and craft a short advertisement using a scarcity tactic. Take into account the following questions as you draft your advertisement:

1. *What urgency phrase will you use to emphasize scarcity?*

2. *How does your ad evoke urgency and make the product feel more desirable?*

3. *Would this ad persuade you to act quickly? Why or why not?*

2.2 Social Proof: Following the Crowd

Have you ever made a decision and felt more assured after seeing others choose the same path? This illustrates the influence of social proof. It is a psychological phenomenon where we look to other people for direction, especially when things are unclear.

For instance, suppose you are looking for dinner while strolling through a new city. You spot two restaurants, one buzzing with locals and the other nearly empty. Which one are you drawn to? Most people would choose the crowded option, interpreting its popularity as a sign of better food or service. This innate tendency to follow the crowd forms the foundation of social proof in advertising.

2.2.1. Why Social Proof Works

Social proof reassures us. We know a product is a good one if other people like it, especially those we admire. Social proof validates our choices and lowers the perceived risk of making the wrong one, whether it be through influencers endorsing a product or positive internet reviews.

2.2.2. Social Proof in Modern Advertising

After learning how social proof works, let us examine the different tactics used by advertisers to build trust and motivate action. These include:

1. **Customer Reviews and Ratings:** The most persuasive forms of social proof are star ratings and internet reviews. This concept is the foundation of websites like Amazon, TripAdvisor, and Yelp, which enable users to share their experiences and help others make wise decisions. A product that has thousands of 5-star reviews, such as the ones given for the Stanley Tumbler (as shown in Figure 2.1), is immediately seen as being trustworthy. Shoppers are more likely to purchase items that appear popular and well-loved by others. By sharing what customers say about a product, potential customers are swayed by their peers' experience versus what the company says.

STANLEY TUMBLER REVIEWS

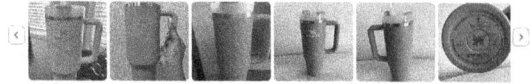

Source: Amazon

2. **Influencer Marketing:** Individuals serve as dependable facilitators for brands and customers, giving their support to goods they recommend. Influencers tend to come out as more relatable than standard celebrity endorsements, which makes their suggestions quite compelling. For example, by working with regular people and micro-influencers who share their candid opinions and experiences, the beauty business, Glossier was able to grow its empire. Because of its genuineness, the brand comes off as personable and reliable, which entices others to test its goods.

3. **Popularity Metrics:** To take advantage of our propensity to follow trends, metrics such as "Bestseller," "Top Rated," or "Most Watched" are shown. The "Top 10" feature on Netflix is a great example of this. Highlighting popular television shows and movies encourages viewers to engage, fostering a sense of urgency and fear of missing out (FOMO), as shown in Figure 2.2. This figure shows

the flyer for the show "Stranger Things". When this show first premiered on Netflix, it quickly captured the spotlight, partly because it was trending as a popular show. It turned into a global sensation fueled by conversations on social media.

Figure 2.2   STRANGER THINGS SHOW FLYER

Source: What's On Netflix

4. **Celebrity and Expert Endorsements:** Celebrities and experts lend their reputation and authority to products, making them more appealing. These endorsements work particularly well in industries like fashion, beauty, and health. For example, Nike's collaborations with athletes like Michael Jordan and Serena Williams combine social proof with authority. The endorsements, such as the one

in Figure 2.3, not only highlight product quality but also associate the brand with excellence and success.

Figure 2.3 SERENA WILLIAMS FOR NIKE

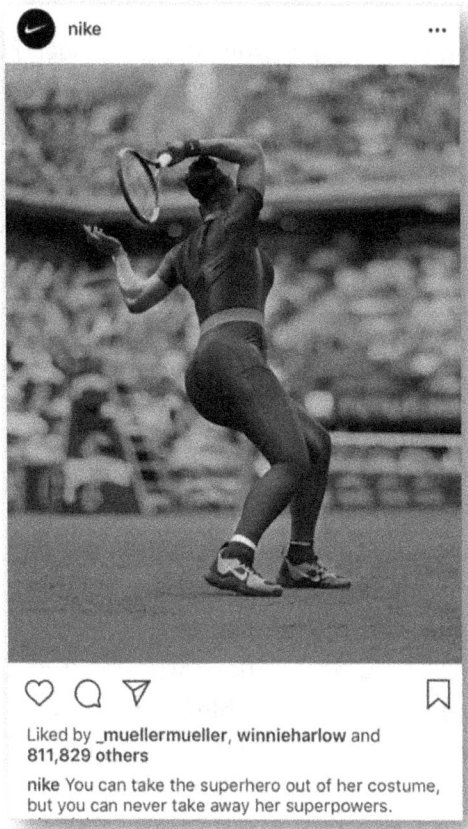

nike

Liked by _muellermueller, winnieharlow and 811,829 others

nike You can take the superhero out of her costume, but you can never take away her superpowers.

Source: (WatsUpTV, 2018)

The effective use of social proof by marketers fosters a sense of community in addition to product sales. Consumers feel part of a shared experience, validated by the choices of others. It's a powerful reminder that in advertising, as in life, people often look to the crowd for direction.

Exercise 2.2: Social Proof

Look for an ad that shows customer reviews or ratings or has someone famous talking about the product. Answer these questions:

a. *Who is supporting or promoting the product? Is it a famous person, an expert, or a regular customer?*

b. *Why do you think seeing this person support the product might make other people want to buy it?*

c. *Does seeing reviews or ratings make you trust the product more? Why?*

2.3 Emotional Appeal: Connecting on a Deeper Level

Emotion is the most powerful advertising method there is. Humans are wired to read and experience emotion, so emotional stories resonate well with us. When advertisers play on our emotions of joy or nostalgia, and even sorrow, that is where they connect with consumers. Emotion-based ads are often the most memorable because they create a connection back to primal experiences and values.

2.3.1. Why Does Emotional Appeal Work?

Our emotions often make our decisions, and then afterward, logic will justify why we made them. When happiness or nostalgia is evoked in emotional triggers, a powerful bond between the consumer and brand results, and this makes for even more effective advertising.

Emotions are crucial in decision-making, according to research by psychologist Antonio Damasio. (Batista, 2011). Strong emotional advertisements are typically more memorable and successful in influencing behavior. Storytelling is a crucial marketing tactic because it allows firms to arouse empathy, which fosters relationships and trust.

2.3.2. Types of Emotional Appeals

1. **Happiness and Positivity:** Ads that make people smile have a higher chance of being shared and remembered. A wonderful instance is Google's "Home Alone" commercial, in which Macaulay Culkin uses humor and nostalgia to reenact sequences from the well-known film in order to promote its Google Assistant device.

2. **Fear and Urgency:** Emphasizing risks can motivate individuals to act, particularly in the context of safety and health initiatives. For instance, anti-smoking advertisements typically employ striking imagery to draw attention to the risks associated with nicotine and instill a sense of urgency to stop smoking.

3. **Belonging and Community:** Loyalty is generated by brands that promote a feeling of community. For instance, Apple's "Think Different" campaign encouraged people to consider themselves as members of a creative elite by celebrating innovators and pioneers.

(You can find the link to watch the videos mentioned in this section on the online resources page.)

Exercise 2.3: Emotional Appeal

Find an ad that makes you feel emotions like happiness or nostalgia (something that reminds you of the past). Then, answer these questions:

a. *What feeling does the ad want you to have? (For example: happy, sad, nostalgic.)*

b. *What parts of the ad make you feel this way?*

c. *How does the ad connect these feelings with the product or brand? Does the emotional message make you like the product more?*

2.4 Authority: Trust the Experts

One very potent psychological principle in advertising is authority. People have an innate tendency to trust others they perceive to be knowledgeable or trustworthy, and this trust frequently extends to the goods and services they endorse. To reassure customers, allay their fears, and increase their self-confidence, advertisers capitalize on this impression of authority. The ambiguity that frequently accompanies decision-making is greatly diminished when a reputable person or group supports a product. This idea works particularly well in industries like health, technology, and finance, where knowledge is essential.

2.4.1. Why Refer to Experts?

Building trust through credibility is the main goal of authority-based advertising. Using phrases like "recommended by doctors," "clinically proven," or "expert-approved" helps customers make decisions.

People frequently seek advice from persons regarded as experts when faced with difficult decisions or novel products. Human psychology is firmly rooted in this reliance on specialists. According to research, people are more likely to purchase a product when it is associated with a reliable person since it implies that the product has undergone extensive testing and validation. A product's attraction is increased when it is linked to authority, and it also lessens any ambiguity or uncertainty that may otherwise cause a buyer to put off making a purchase.

2.4.2. Examples of Authority in Advertising

Businesses in a variety of sectors use authority in various ways to build consumer confidence and bolster their messaging:

1. **Expert Recommendations:** The legitimacy of the product is increased by showcasing experts in the field, such as physicians or scientists. For example, Sensodyne toothpaste ads prominently feature dentists recommending the product for individuals with sensitive teeth. This association not only validates the product but also positions it as the leading solution in its category.

2. **Certifications and Awards:** Communicating certifications or awards gives the product more legitimacy by demonstrating that it has undergone stringent testing or received approval from relevant organizations. For instance, in the case of wine, the medal signifies quality and importance, so wine bottles featuring the label "Gold Medal Winner—International Wine Competition" immediately attract consumers' attention.

3. **Data-Driven Advertising:** Using precise data and statistics strengthens credibility and reassures consumers that the product is effective. An example is Proactiv's skincare ads, which frequently cite dermatological studies, claiming "80% of users saw clearer skin within two weeks." These statistics appeal to logical reasoning, giving consumers tangible proof of the product's efficacy.

2.4.3. Authority in the Digital Age

The Internet has amplified the impact of authority in advertising. Today, brands don't just rely on traditional experts; they also turn to influencers and content creators who have cultivated authority within specific niches.

For instance:

- **Tech Influencers:** Marques Brownlee (MKBHD) reviews gadgets with a level of detail that positions him as an authority in consumer electronics. Brands like Google and Apple collaborate with him to introduce their latest products. Watch his review of the iPhone 15 through the link provided on our online resource page.

- **Health and Wellness Bloggers:** Registered dietitians or fitness coaches with strong online followings promote supplements, workout programs, or meal plans, blending personal relatability with professional credibility.

This shift reflects a democratization of authority, where expertise isn't limited to formal qualifications but also includes earned trust within a community.

Exercise 2.4: Using Authority in Ads

Look at the fictional advertisement provided and answer the questions below.

a. *Who is endorsing this product in the ad?*

b. *Does the recommendation from dentists make you trust the product more? Why?*

In Conclusion

By concentrating on the psychological aspects that impact consumer behavior, companies can create advertising techniques that work. Scarcity, authority, emotional appeal, and social proof all have a big influence on how people make decisions because they appeal to basic human instincts like connection, urgency, trust, and validation.

Understanding these ideas will help brands create campaigns that connect with consumers, build trust, and encourage steadfast loyalty. Knowing the motivations behind our purchases, whether it's the thrill of scarcity or the confidence built by professional recommendations, enables marketers to develop effective, customer-focused strategies that produce outcomes.

Chapter Summary

- Time-limited promotions and low-stock alerts are particularly effective because scarcity heightens urgency and value perception by appealing to the fear of missing out (FOMO).

- Social proof illustrates what other people are doing to change behavior through techniques like customer evaluations, popularity measurements, and influencer endorsements.

- Emotional appeal develops strong feelings and lasting impressions by involving listeners on a personal level through the use of storytelling, joy, fear, or nostalgia.

- Authority gives consumers peace of mind when they are making decisions by establishing trust through expert endorsements, certifications, and data-driven claims.

- Apple exemplifies these principles by creating anticipation through scarcity, validating its products with social proof, connecting emotionally through creative campaigns, and reinforcing its reputation with expert reviews and awards.

- In order to increase consumer confidence and loyalty and boost product sales, effective advertising makes use of these psychological concepts.

Quiz

1. **What psychological principle explains why limited-time offers are effective?**
   a. Social proof
   b. Authority
   c. Scarcity
   d. Emotional appeal

2. **What fear does scarcity advertising often tap into?**
   a. Fear of failure
   b. Fear of missing out (FOMO)
   c. Fear of authority
   d. Fear of rejection

3. **Why do people trust products that display "doctor recommended" labels?**
   a. Because of social proof
   b. Because of emotional appeal
   c. Because of scarcity
   d. Because of authority

4. **What is social proof?**
   a. Using expert endorsements to build trust
   b. Influencing people by showcasing what others are doing
   c. Highlighting limited availability to create urgency
   d. Using emotions to connect with consumers

5. **Which advertising method uses customer testimonials and reviews?**
   a. Emotional appeal
   b. Scarcity
   c. Social proof
   d. Authority

6. **In advertising, what is an example of emotional appeal?**
   a. A heartfelt ad showing a family celebrating together
   b. A limited-edition product announcement
   c. A product labeled "#1 recommended by experts"
   d. An influencer promoting a product on social media

7. **Why is emotional appeal effective in advertising?**
   a. It bypasses logical decision-making and connects with feelings.
   b. It ensures customers act immediately.
   c. It highlights expert endorsements.
   d. It validates a product's popularity.

8. **What type of social proof does Netflix use with its "Top 10" feature?**
   a. Authority
   b. Emotional appeal
   c. Customer testimonials
   d. Popularity metrics

9. What is the role of influencers in social proof advertising?
   a. To limit the availability of a product
   b. To act as relatable spokespeople and endorse products
   c. To evoke emotional responses through storytelling
   d. To provide expert recommendations

10. What is loss aversion?
   a. The fear of choosing the wrong product
   b. The tendency to avoid losses rather than seek gains
   c. The belief that others know better
   d. The avoidance of emotional connections in advertising

Answers

1 – c	2 – b	3 – d	4 – b	5 – c
6 – a	7 – a	8 – d	9 – b	10 – b

Case Study: Apple's Masterclass in Marketing Psychology

One of the big reasons for Apple's status as a cultural icon is the way the company uses, in really clever ways, various psychological concepts to advertise. It exploits concepts such as scarcity, social proof, emotional appeal, and authority in creating advertising campaigns that do so much more than sell products.

Creating Urgency and Anticipation

One of Apple's most successful strategies is scarcity. The company wants to create a sense of overwhelming demand when introducing new products. Apple increases interest in their products by limiting the initial availability and pre-order window.

This is a deliberate strategy to give Apple products a feeling of exclusivity and luxury. When new iPhone models are released, for instance, the lines outside Apple stores reflect not only genuine demand but also enhance Apple's brand. Because of the heightened excitement surrounding a product's release, every purchase feels like a victory for the buyer.

The Power of the Collective

Apple knows people trust what others recommend, and they use that to their advantage. The "Shot on iPhone" campaign is a great example. By using real photos and videos from customers, Apple shows off the creative capabilities of its products. Besides features, they tell the story of how regular people can achieve amazing things with an iPhone.

Apple also uses influential voices to amplify social proof. Collaborations with filmmakers, photographers, and musicians show off the device and link the brand to excellence. A great example is Billie Eilish's music video for

"Your Power," which was shot entirely on an iPhone and blends art and product perfectly.

Beyond individual users, Apple's community building amplifies social proof. The crazy things developers are doing with the Apple ecosystem at the WWDC are shown to customers, and they feel part of something bigger.

Connecting Through Meaningful Stories

Apple doesn't just sell devices; it sells experiences, emotions, and connections. The core of the company's advertising is storytelling, and that resonates deeply with its audience.

Take the "Shot on iPhone" campaign. The images are technically impressive, but what makes them powerful is the focus on capturing life's biggest moments: family gatherings, adventures, or everyday beauty. These ads show an iPhone as a tool to record and save memories.

Apple's continuous "Think Different" campaign embodies this emotional connection. It celebrates individuality, inventiveness, and the courage to break the rules. Apple connects with people who can relate to that story by surrounding themselves with inventors, dreamers, and visionaries.

Even the simplicity of Apple's ads is key. No technical mumbo jumbo. Just how their products make life better.

The Confidence of Innovation

Apple has a strong reputation for design and technology, which strengthens the brand's appeal. The company's pioneering history, which includes revolutionary technologies like the M1 microprocessor, Face ID, and the Retina Display, makes it stand out as a pioneer in its field.

Through industry recognition and professional recommendations, the business strengthens this authority. Apple consistently incorporates accolades like "Best Smartphone of the Year" or quotations from reputable tech publications like TechRadar and The Verge. These suggestions reassure the buyer because they are certain that the product they are purchasing has previously been proven to be high-quality and effective.

The same goes for the product demonstrations. When an executive such as Craig Federighi or Tim Cook presents at an Apple event, their confidence in delivery and attention to detail give credibility to the products being unveiled.

Apple does a great job of weaving all these concepts into a cohesive strategy. Scarcity creates excitement and urgency; social proof builds trust and community; emotional appeal creates a personal connection; and authority enhances confidence. Combined, these elements make the marketing campaigns by Apple both memorable and effective.

The real strength of Apple's approach is in the insight that the customers are investing in a brand that touches their aspirations, creativity, and identity. Apple sets expectations, turning every interaction into an opportunity to build loyalty and admiration.

Source: (Clinehens, 2022)

Exercise: Ad Psychology in Action

Create an ad for a fictional product using at least two of the psychological principles covered in this chapter. For example, you could:

- *Highlight scarcity with a "limited-time offer" banner.*
- *Incorporate social proof by including testimonials or ratings from satisfied customers.*

Further Learning

Links also available in Online Resources:

1. **Examples of ads for section 2.3.2 –Types of Emotional Appeals:**

   a. **Example of happiness and positivity: Home Alone Ad**
      http://bit.ly/4IGLnPF

   b. **Example of fear and urgency: CDC Anti-smoking Ad**
      http://bit.ly/44JZcaj

   c. **Example of belonging and community: Apple- Think Different**
      http://bit.ly/4o7hEBm

2. **iPhone 15 review by Marques Brownlee: Marques Brownlee**
   http://bit.ly/4fn7oRz

CHAPTER 3
Building an Advertising Strategy

Key Learning Objectives

- How to identify and comprehend your target group to create messaging that has a greater impact.
- The significance of establishing precise, quantifiable advertising objectives.
- Why a successful plan relies on data and how to collect and use it.
- How to perform a SWOT analysis
- Nike's method for connecting with its audience and its advertising campaign.

Every successful campaign starts with a strong advertising strategy. Think of it as the blueprint that transforms creative ideas into impactful results. Without it, even the most eye-catching ads risk falling flat, failing to connect with the right audience, or achieving meaningful results. A robust strategy ensures all campaign elements work together to engage, influence, and leave a lasting impression.

3.1 Who's Your Target Audience?

Your key focus in your marketing is your target audience. Meredith Hill, a prominent figure in the travel industry known for empowering travel professionals and entrepreneurs, expresses a notion along the lines of: "If you talk to everyone, then you're actually talking to nobody." (MIC MEDIA, 2021) This is why targeting and understanding your audience segment in the context of your message is very important. Speaking to the wrong audience is like throwing a fishing line in a desert — no matter what words you use, your ad buys won't be effective, no matter how good they are.

3.1.1 Why Defining Your Audience Matters

Having the idea of the audience in your mind's eye is beneficial in order to have a more appealing and practical concept that ultimately increases your chances of making the sale. Creating a mesh between your product and the audience's requirements is closely related to having a sense of appreciation and understanding, which is the best precursor for a deeper connection. The stronger the connection the audience has with your brand, the better their chances of turning into devoted customers.

With a clear strategy, you can help encourage tailored communication that speaks to what they are interested in. Typical appeals directed toward everyone usually have low chances of stirring activity because the threshold engagement is absent. The goal should be to craft messages that talk to and resonate with particular people as opposed to talking to everyone and throwing everything at the wall.

3.1.2 How to Identify Your Target Audience

To gain a deeper insight into how to identify your target audience, it is prudent to consider psychological triggers influencing consumer behavior. A research paper by Coulter and Roggeveen (2012) titled 'The Impact of Urgency on Advertising Effectiveness' found that advertisements employing symbols of urgency, such as 'limited time only' or countdown clocks, were much more effective compared to those not employing such symbols. In fact, sales increased by a further 30% following urgency advertisements, showing the incredible power of engaging individuals with time-based messages.

Some of the steps to identify your target audience are:

1. **Segment Your Market**

   Split your audience into sets based on some of the most important demographics:

   - **Demographics:** Age, gender, income, education, and location
   - **Psychographics:** Lifestyles, values, interests, and attitudes.
   - **Behavior:** Brand loyalty, purchasing habits, and engagement preferences.
   - **Geographics:** Targeting based on climate, urban/rural settings, or even neighborhood trends.
   - **Technographics:** The platforms and tools your audience utilizes—a smartphone, tablet, or desktop.

2. **Build Buyer Personas**

   Develop detailed profiles of your ideal customers to guide your strategy. Buyer personas make your audience feel real, allowing you to tailor your messaging to their unique needs and preferences. Figure 3.1 below is an example of a user persona for a Green Gen Z audience, detailing specifics such as age, gender, interests, goals, and pain points that will allow for targeted communication based on her persona.

Figure 3.1 SAMPLE USER PERSONA

Sarah Chen

Green Gen Z

I don't need to relocate to Mars. I need businesses and brands to help protect the Earth.

DEMOGRAPHICS
- **Age:** 22
- **Gender:** Female
- **Location:** Oakland, CA
- **Occupation:** Recent Graduate

INTERESTS

Sustainable Fashion   Eco-Friendly Products

Environmental Activism

GOALS
- Find brands that prioritize sustainability
- Reduce personal carbon footprint
- Connect with environmentally conscious communities

⚠ **PAIN POINTS**
- Limited budget for sustainable products
- Difficulty verifying genuine eco-friendly claims
- Lack of accessible, sustainable options

3. **Analyze Competitors**

Keep an eye on the competition's tactics and the precise people they are aiming at. Look for the spaces that they haven't closed. You can start with your brand if a travel gear firm is focusing on families and neglecting the millennials who have become digital nomads along the road.

3.1.3 Pinpoint the Audience's Emotional Triggers

Recollecting what we learned in Chapter 2, understanding the emotional factors driving your audience's decisions is essential for effective marketing. Buying decisions are frequently driven by emotions and then justified afterward. Pay attention to their pain points (like worries about budgeting for a financial app), aspirations (such as the desire for exclusivity with luxury brands), and fears (for instance, concerns about data security with antivirus software).

3.1.4 Map Their Customer Journey

Before creating your message, you need to understand where your audience is in their decision-making process. Like any journey, customers move through distinct stages, each requiring different types of communication according to their needs. Developing and delivering an effective strategy means that you will be able to have the right conversation at the right time, which will translate to sales. The customer journey typically involves three stages, which are discussed below:

- **Awareness:** The customer becomes aware of a need or problem. At this stage, your role as an advertiser is to be informative rather than promotional. Focus on education and problem-solving to build credibility and trust. This is where the principle of authority becomes crucial. For example, if you're advertising skincare products, share expert tips about acne prevention rather than pushing your product directly. This approach positions your brand as a helpful authority and acknowledges that customers in this stage are seeking information, and are not necessarily ready to buy.

- **Consideration:** At this stage, the customer is evaluating solutions. Your role as an advertiser is to ensure that you highlight your product or service's benefits and features and enable your customer to make some form of comparison. This is when social proof becomes particularly powerful; your ad may include reviews showcasing why your product outperforms competitors, thus making the competition irrelevant. Remember that people tend to follow the crowd, so highlighting your existing customer base can significantly influence decision-making.

- **Decision:** In this phase, the customer chooses a product or service. This is where leveraging multiple psychology principles becomes essential. For example, you can reinforce trust with testimonials (authority and social proof), provide a limited-time offer (scarcity), or use a different combination suited to your context. "Buy now and save x%" is a common tactic that prompts immediate action by combining urgency with a clear value proposition.

Notice how the advertising approach progresses strategically from education (awareness) to comparison (consideration) to action (decision). This progression aligns with how customers naturally make purchasing decisions.

3.1.5 Leverage Behavioral Data

Understanding the customer journey stages becomes even more powerful when combined with behavioral data. Digital platforms allow us to observe how customers interact with our content and advertising at each stage, providing valuable insights for refining our approach.

Different behaviors signal different stages in the customer journey. For instance, when potential customers are reading blog posts about acne prevention, they're likely in the awareness stage. Once they start comparing products and reading reviews, they've moved to consideration. Activities like adding items to the cart or searching for coupon codes indicate they're in the decision stage.

By matching these observable behaviors to journey stages, we can create more relevant, timely advertising that meets customers exactly where they are. This data-driven approach helps ensure our messaging evolution aligns with the customer's actual journey, not just our assumptions about it.

Table 3.1 below, which uses our skincare example, summarizes the customer's journey stages, showing how the customer mindset evolves, what messages resonate best, and which behaviors to watch for at each phase.

Table 3.1 DEVELOPING MESSAGING BASED ON THE CUSTOMER JOURNEY PHASE

	Awareness Stage	Consideration Stage	Decision Stage
Customer Mindset	"I might have a problem."	"What are my options?"	"I'm ready to buy!"
Message Focus	Education and problem-solving	Highlight benefits, features, and comparisons.	Reinforce trust with testimonials or limited-time offers
Sample Message	*Struggling with acne? Discover 5 prevention tips from dermatologists.*	*"95% of users saw clearer skin in 4 weeks. See why our formula works better."*	*"Join 10,000+ happy customers. Save 20% on your first purchase today!"*
Observable Behavior	• Blog post views • Social media engagement • Newsletter signups	• Product page visits • Review section clicks • Comparison tool usage	• Cart additions • Coupon code searches • Store locator usage

3.1.6 Example: Dove's Campaign for Real Beauty

Dove defied the standards of beauty in advertising by showcasing actual women in all shapes, sizes, ages, and ethnicities, similar to what regular people, not professional models, see in the mirror. The public realized that there is no one-size-fits-all definition of beauty because everyone has a unique experience creating their conception. Watch the video through the link available on the online resources page.

Exercise 3.1: Define Your Target Audience

A new line of eco-friendly water bottles called EcoFlow, for people who are conscious about the environment and always on the go, is preparing for launch. Answer the following questions to define your audience.

1. **Demographics:**

    - *What age group are you targeting?*
    - *What is their income level?*
    - *Where do they live (urban, suburban, or rural)?*

2. **Psychographics:**

    - *What values or lifestyles does your audience embrace?*
    - *Are they health-conscious, environmentally aware, or both?*

3. **Behavior:**

    - *How does your audience shop (online, in-store, or both)?*
    - *What kind of brands or products do they currently use?*

---

4. **Create a Persona:**

- *Combine the above details to create a buyer persona. Example:*
- *Name: Green Greg*
- *Age: 28*
- *Lifestyle: Fitness enthusiast and environmental advocate*
- *Goal: Prefers sustainable and reusable products for daily use*

Write a 2–3 sentence description of your target audience.

3.2 Setting Goals That Make Sense (And You Can Measure)

Goals are the foundation of any successful advertising strategy; they should include a built-in campaign plan that outlines how to take ideas from inception to completion. Even the most creative campaigns can go awry without achievable objectives, wasting money and failing to achieve their intended outcome. Setting goals helps your company stay focused and ensures that all decisions, from messages to whether or not to use PPC, will support your high-level objectives.

To ensure goals are clear and effective, the SMART framework serves as a proven guide. This methodology ensures that your goals are:

1. **Specific:** Vague goals like "increase sales" or "boost brand awareness" can lead to scattered efforts. A specific goal

zeroes in on exactly what you want to achieve. Specificity leaves no room for ambiguity, helping teams stay aligned and purposeful.

Example: "Increase website traffic by 20% through targeted social media ads."

2. **Measurable:** What is measured gets managed. When you measure your goals, you can track where you stand and measure success. Metrics can include:

- Click-through rates (CTR)
- Conversion rates
- Sales figures
- Metrics for engagement: likes, shares, comments

Example: "Achieve a 15% increase in Instagram engagement over the next two months."

3. **Achievable:** Set challenging yet attainable goals that fit within your budget, time commitment, and available resources.

Example: "Increase revenue by 10% in three months through targeted email campaigns."

4. **Relevant:** Goals must align with your overall business objectives. Ask yourself: Does this goal contribute to the larger mission or vision?

Example: A brand aiming to build brand awareness may focus on increasing social media followers rather than immediate sales.

5. **Time-bound:** Deadlines create urgency and help maintain momentum. A time-bound goal provides a clear timeline, ensuring that tasks don't drag on indefinitely.

   Example: "Increase YouTube subscribers by 25% within three months."

You can see this framework illustrated in Figure 3.2.

Figure 3.2 **SMART GOAL FRAMEWORK**

- Specific
- Measurable
- Achievable
- Relevant
- Time-bound

Here is another example:

Goal: Launch a campaign to promote a new fitness app.

- **Specific:** Increase app downloads.
- **Measurable:** Achieve 10,000 downloads.

- **Achievable:** Partner with influencers to target fitness enthusiasts.
- **Relevant:** Aligns with the brand's goal to dominate the digital fitness space.
- **Time-bound:** Achieve the target within three months.

3.2.1. Why the SMART Framework Works

The SMART framework makes goals simple enough for team members to follow and turn into concrete actions, which removes uncertainty and holds people accountable. Let us see a SMART goal in action below.

3.2.2 Example: IKEA's Lamp 2 Campaign

IKEA's Lamp 2 campaign exemplifies the power of a SMART goal in action. Within a year, the brand aimed to establish sustainability as a key component of its identity. The campaign focused on eco-warrior ideas and included themed benefits such as why you should reuse and recycle items, along with some creativity and an emotional connection.

IKEA demonstrated its support for green issues and connected with environmentally conscious consumers by connecting itself with sustainable practices. This prompted readers to consider sustainability in their everyday lives. Watch the video through the link provided on the online resources page.

Exercise 3.2: Create Two SMART Goals

Using the information from Exercise 3.1, create two SMART campaign goals that follow the framework:

1. **Specific:** *Define what you want to achieve.*
2. **Measurable:** *Include a quantifiable metric.*
3. **Achievable:** *Ensure that it is realistic.*
4. **Relevant:** *Align with the campaign's objectives.*
5. **Time-bound:** *Set a deadline.*

3.3 Doing Your Research: Why Data Is Everything

Data ensures that your efforts are well-informed and productive by acting as the strategy's compass. It helps you understand your audience's identity, behavior, and decision-making factors by converting uncertainty into precision. Data provides useful insights that help campaigns achieve their objectives effectively and efficiently, from determining your target audience to improving results.

3.3.1. Why Data Matters

Data is the cornerstone of informed decision-making, cutting through ambiguity to bring precision and clarity to advertising strategies. It empowers advertisers to understand their audience, allocate resources efficiently, and measure success with confidence. Even the most creative campaigns risk falling flat without the guidance of data, leading to wasted time, effort, and budget. Data assists in:

- **Enhancing Audience Insight:** Detailed information about your audience's preferences allows you to craft campaigns that truly resonate and differentiate themselves.

- **Campaign Enhancement:** Performance data reveals which strategies are effective and which are not, enabling you to implement real-time adjustments that maintain the effectiveness of your campaigns.

- **Boosting ROI:** Making data-driven decisions focuses resources on the most effective strategies, maximizing returns, and ensuring that every investment significantly contributes to your goals.

3.3.2. Types of Data in Advertising

To develop an effective advertising strategy, you need to understand and use different types of data. Each type gives you unique insights about your audience and helps you shape your campaign. By using these types of data together, as illustrated in Table 3.2, you can better understand your audience's story and create campaigns that connect, influence, and drive results.

Table 3.2 TYPES OF DATA USED IN STRATEGY

	Demographic	Behavioral	Psychographic	Performance
What the Data Answers	Who are they?	How do they act?	What do they care about?	How effective is the campaign?
The Data We Use	Age Gender Location Income	Time spent online, Preferred content types, Shopping habits, Platform usage	Interests Values Lifestyle Attitudes	Click-through rates, Engagement metrics, Conversion rates, Return on Investment (ROI)
How the Data Informs Strategy	Knowing the audience is essential for targeted messaging. It impacts many elements of the strategy.	Tells us where and how to reach them.	Guides content themes and messaging.	Shows what content works best.
Example	*The target audience of a luxury watch brand would be 30s to 50s urban professionals working in large cities.*	*Amazon tracks past purchases to recommend products that align with a user's buying habits, boosting sales through personalization.*	*Patagonia appeals to environmentally conscious consumers by emphasizing sustainability and ethical production in its campaigns.*	*A brand launching a social media campaign uses ROI data to determine if ad spend resulted in profitable conversions.*

Note: For a comprehensive exploration of performance metrics, measurement tools, and data analysis techniques, see Chapter 9.

Let us learn more about each type of data in a bit more detail:

- **Demographic Data:** Demographics tell you the basic facts about your audience, like their age, gender, income, and location. Ask yourself, are you targeting Gen Z (individuals born between 1997–2012), Millennials (individuals born between 1981–1996), or Baby Boomers (individuals born between 1946–1964)? How does your product appeal to different genders? Can your audience afford it based on their income level? Are they urban dwellers or rural residents? Answering these questions helps you focus your efforts on the right people.

- **Behavioral Data:** Behavioral data is concerned with what your audience does: their habits, preferences, and interactions. Questions to consider include how often they shop, what types of content they engage with online, if they are loyal to specific brands, or if they frequently try new ones. These insights tell you where and how to reach them, making your advertising efforts more precise and impactful.

- **Psychographic Data:** Psychographics reveal your audience's motivations, values, and interests, the "why" behind their actions. Think about what inspires your audience: Are they driven by convenience, status, or self-expression? Are they environmentally conscious, adventurous, or family-oriented? Understanding these factors helps you create campaigns that resonate on a deeper level, aligning your message with their core beliefs.

- **Performance Data:** Performance data evaluates how well your campaigns are doing. Metrics like click-through rates (CTR), conversion rates, and return on investment (ROI) tell you what's working and what's not. For example, CTR reveals how many people clicked on your ad, while ROI shows whether your investment paid off. This data is essential for refining your strategy and ensuring your efforts drive meaningful results.

3.4 SWOT Analysis: Your Brand's Strengths and Weaknesses

Knowing your brand's current position and leveraging its strengths, weaknesses, and opportunities while putting a strong strategy in place to counteract any threats is made possible via SWOT analysis. Businesses may stay competitive in the market, outmaneuver even scale changes, and make goal-driven investment decisions by using this systematic SWOT analysis process.

3.4.1. Why Conduct a SWOT Analysis?

- A SWOT analysis provides a comprehensive snapshot of internal and external factors that influence your brand, giving you clarity for your strategy.
- It enables informed decision-making. By highlighting particular areas to focus on, the plan remains proactive rather than reactive in the future.
- The goal of strengths and opportunities is to concentrate on the resources that will most likely benefit everyone.
- Your brand can steer clear of difficulties, obstacles, and rivals by being aware of threats and weaknesses.

3.4.2. How to Conduct a SWOT Analysis

1. **Strengths: Leverage Your Advantages**

   Determine what makes your brand unique in the marketplace. Consider elements like:

- **Brand Reputation:** Is your company known and trustworthy in your sector?
- **Unique Products and Services:** Do your goods and services offer creative answers to current problems?
- **Operational Efficiency:** Have you been able to improve quality or minimize costs through simplifying your processes?

Example: Tesla, as a leader in electric vehicles and sustainable technology, is differentiating itself through its cutting-edge technology & innovative looks.

2. **Weaknesses: Address Internal Challenges**

   Pinpoint areas where your brand needs improvement to better compete. Ask if there are gaps in your product lineup or service offerings, or if you struggle with customer satisfaction or delivery issues. Finally, ask if your pricing strategy is competitive.

   Example: While known for quality, Tesla has faced criticism for delays in delivery timelines, which can impact customer trust.

3. **Opportunities: Leverage External Trends**

   Identify market, technological, or consumer trends that will help you build your brand. Think about untapped markets or emerging markets to sell in. Is there a growing market for products similar to yours as a result of technological or cultural changes? Do partnerships or collaborations increase your visibility?

   Example: Beyond Meat (and other plant-based food companies) have certainly illustrated that the uptick in interest in both sustainability and nutrition-focused food options can be profitable.

4. Threats: Prepare for External Challenges

Evaluate factors outside your control that could hinder success. Think about:

- Increased competition or market saturation.
- Economic downturns or changes in consumer spending habits.
- Evolving regulations or environmental challenges.

Example: Ride-sharing companies like Uber face threats from stricter regulations and growing competition from similar platforms.

Figure 3.3 illustrates a SWOT analysis framework.

Figure 3.3 SWOT ANALYSIS FRAMEWORK

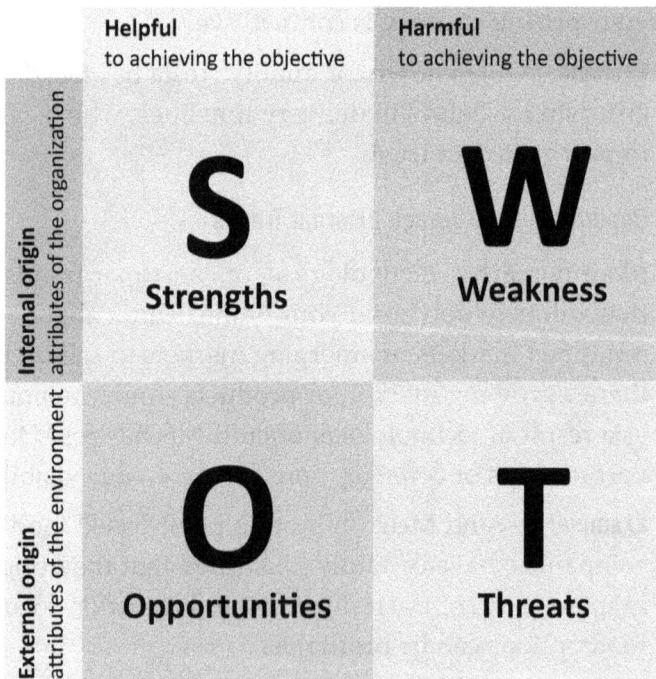

	Helpful to achieving the objective	Harmful to achieving the objective
Internal origin attributes of the organization	**S** Strengths	**W** Weakness
External origin attributes of the environment	**O** Opportunities	**T** Threats

3.4.3. Steps for Effective SWOT Analysis

1. **Gather Data:** Use internal reports, market research, customer insights, and competitive scans to inform the evaluation.

2. **Get Their Take:** Get input from each department to ensure a more holistic view of all the strengths, weaknesses, opportunities, and threats.

3. **Rank Priorities:** Not all parts of your SWOT analysis will be of equal importance; it is critical to recognise which ones are.

4. **Develop Strategies:** Use the findings to craft actionable plans. For example:

    *   Match strengths to opportunities to maximize potential.

    *   Address weaknesses to minimize threats.

Exercise 3.3: Develop a SWOT Analysis for a Local Coffee Shop

Business Description: A friendly and welcoming coffee shop that serves the requirements of students and young professionals is privately owned and is located in a busy downtown location. It offers artisanal coffee, pastries, and free Wi-Fi.

a. *Fill out a SWOT diagram for the above fictional business.*

b. *Provide a short paragraph analyzing key findings and providing recommendations for the business.*

In Conclusion

In order to ensure that the right people will hear your message, one of the most crucial aspects of creating a successful advertising strategy is to choose a target audience. Establishing success criteria and staying on course are two benefits of setting measurable goals.

Data analysis and in-depth research produce useful knowledge that enhances decision-making. An effective SWOT analysis also helps you assess your brand's position by examining its opportunities, threats, weaknesses, and strengths.

These elements work together to give marketers a roadmap for developing campaigns that are both captivating and strategically sound, enabling them to seize opportunities and get over challenges in a competitive market.

Chapter Summary

- Finding your target audience: Knowing who you are targeting allows you to craft messaging that will resonate with the right people and invite real engagement.

- SMART Goal Framework: Time-bound goals (tied to what is measurable), relevant to the campaign, Specific and Achievable give campaigns direction and clarity.

- Data-Driven Decisions: Using this data to see what tactics are working and make in-the-moment adjustments means you increase chances for better results.

- SWOT Analysis: Analyzes an organization's opportunities, threats, weaknesses, and strengths; actually makes strategic positioning and risk reduction easier.

- Audience Segmentation: You can increase the relevance of your ads and viewers at various levels by segmenting them.

- Performance tracking: Allows for future campaign decision-making by tracking what is effective.

- Strategic Planning: Align campaigns with company goals to ensure consistency and quantifiable improvement.

Quiz

1. **Why is identifying your target audience important?**
   - a. To save money on production
   - b. To ensure messaging connects effectively
   - c. To focus solely on demographic data
   - d. To avoid using SMART goals

2. **What does the "S" in SMART goals stand for?**
   - a. Specific
   - b. Simple
   - c. Strategic
   - d. Standardized

3. **Which of the corresponding answer choices is an example of a good SMART goal?**
   - a. Increase sales soon
   - b. Be the best brand in the market
   - c. Achieve a 10% revenue increase in 6 months through social media campaigns
   - d. Reach more customers

4. **What type of data explains *why* your audience behaves a certain way?**
   - a. Demographic data
   - b. Behavioral data
   - c. Psychographic data
   - d. Performance data

5. **Which tool is best for tracking website traffic and user behavior?**
   a. Canva
   b. HubSpot
   c. MailChimp
   d. Google Analytics

6. **What is the primary benefit of data in marketing campaigns?**
   a. It drives informed decision-making and refinement
   b. It prevents campaigns from failing entirely
   c. It eliminates the need for creativity
   d. It prevents campaigns from failing entirely

7. **What does the "T" in SWOT analysis stand for?**
   a. Time
   b. Threats
   c. Techniques
   d. Trends

8. **Which of the following is a strength in SWOT analysis?**
   a. A competitor's strong brand presence
   b. Your company's innovative product
   c. Limited marketing budget
   d. Industry regulations

9. **How does performance data benefit campaigns?**
   a. It ensures goals are SMART
   b. It focuses on competitor trends
   c. It identifies audience demographics
   d. It highlights what's working and allows for real-time adjustments

10. **What is the key characteristic of a "time-bound" goal?**
    a. It is achievable within a set period
    b. It focuses on performance metrics
    c. It is aligned with data analysis
    d. It is relevant to a brand's mission

Answers

1 – b	2 – a	3 – c	4 – c	5 – d
6 – a	7 – b	8 – b	9 – d	10 – a

Case Study: Nike's Dream Crazy Campaign

In 2018, Nike took a big, bold, and polarizing stance with the Dream Crazy campaign, centered around Colin Kaepernick (now a former NFL player and one-time protestor, opting to simply kneel during the national anthem in hopes more people noticed). It centered around the hashtag **"Believe in something."** Even if that's all you need to believe in, Nike came across as 'bravery, equality, activism' as a result, which was consistent with the brand's objective to inspire athletes and, in a little way, change the world.

This campaign received a lot of media attention and demonstrated how well-placed intent can align a brand with the aspirations, ambitions, and values of its community, creating a significant cultural effect.

Understanding the Audience

This is where Nike excelled in knowing and inspiring its core audience (young socially conscious Millennials + Gen Z, primarily). They lean toward brands that are creating change on important issues, like racial justice and equality. Psychographic insights led us to believe that Nike's core audience desired an authentic and purpose-driven narrative, making "Dream Crazy" the next right thing for the brand.

By syncing its messaging with this alignment, Nike solidified its credibility as a market leader, taking risks and speaking out on important cultural issues.

Aligning with Audience Values

The marketing capitalized on a time when companies had more meaning than just making money. The Kaepernick visual was a message that resonated with emotions, placing Nike in the camp of risk-taking, activism, and resiliency. It emotionally engages with people, encouraging them to pursue their goals regardless of obstacles. This link strengthened Nike's brand purpose by going beyond aspiration to include a call to action for social justice.

In order to further ground the message in authenticity, the campaign also made use of Nike's long-standing affiliation with players like LeBron James and Serena Williams, who represent bravery and tenacity.

Execution and Creative Strategy

"Dream Crazy" launched as a multimedia campaign, utilizing platforms like YouTube, Twitter, Instagram, and traditional television to maximize visibility. Its centerpiece was a powerful two-minute video featuring Kaepernick alongside athletes who had overcome significant personal and professional challenges. The emotionally charged narrative was bolstered by a wholly digital-first strategy to capture the target audience's attention, which consisted of tech-savvy Nike fanatics.

The campaign's reach and relevance were increased by the celebrity endorsements, and it became a cultural topic thanks to the chatter on social media, TV, and traditional advertising. By positioning the campaign as a movement, Nike successfully tied its message to larger societal shifts.

Measurable Impact

In spite of early controversy, which included conservative groups' condemnation and boycotts, the campaign was a huge financial and cultural success.

- **Sales Boom:** Within days of the campaign's debut, Nike's sales rose by 31%. Potential risks were transformed into significant returns as the brand's strong language struck a chord with its target audience.

- **Boost Brand Value:** Nike's stock reached its peak soon after the ad launched, indicating that investors supported their approach.

- **Cultural Relevance:** The campaign garnered multiple accolades, including an Emmy for Outstanding Commercial, and established Nike as the industry leader in purpose marketing.

- **Social Media Engagement:** This marketing video went viral in a matter of hours, garnering millions of views and causing the hashtag #Justdo_it to trend globally, demonstrating Nike's dominance in digital culture.

SWOT Analysis of the Campaign

STRENGTHS	WEAKNESSES
The campaign's bold messaging reinforced Nike's alignment with progressive values, fostering loyalty among younger, socially conscious consumers. Its high-profile celebrity endorsements added credibility and appeal.	The politically charged nature of the campaign alienated a segment of Nike's audience, particularly conservative customers.
OPPORTUNITIES	**THREATS**
The growing demand for purpose-driven brands allowed Nike to capture cultural relevance and market share by taking a strong social stance.	The polarizing nature of the campaign exposed Nike to boycotts and potential reputational risks, as not all segments of its audience supported the messaging.

Lessons from Nike's Success

- **Authenticity = Connection:** Nike created an emotional resonance that went beyond the aforementioned criticism by tying brand ideals with audience goals.

- **Emotional Purpose-Driven Marketing Lands:** It set Nike apart from its rivals and made marketing and the market responsible for making a statement.

- **Bold Risks Can Pay Off:** Strategic planning and deep audience understanding enabled Nike to transform a polarizing decision into measurable success.

By strategically planning and aligning its campaign with the values of its audience, Nike not only achieved remarkable financial results but also cemented its role as a culturally relevant brand championing change. Watch the campaign through the link on our online resources page.

Source: (The Brand Hopper, 2024)

Exercise: Create a Mini Ad Strategy

Choose a fictional product and complete these steps:

1. *Define the target audience, creating a buyer persona.*
2. *Set a SMART goal for your campaign.*
3. *Collect one key piece of data to inform your strategy.*
4. *Conduct a brief SWOT analysis for the brand.*

Further Learning

Links also available in Online Resources:

1. **Dove ad for section 3.1.5: Dove Real Beauty Sketches**
   http://bit.ly/3TVaxhw
2. **Ikea video for SMART goals: IKEA Lamp Commercial**
   https://bit.ly/4m2hQ2M
3. **Nike case study campaign video: Nike Dream Crazy Campaign**
   http://bit.ly/4o2SK5C

CHAPTER 4

Clicks, Likes, and Conversions

Key Learning Objectives

- How to identify and leverage key platforms for your brand's unique goals.
- The importance of tailoring content to specific platforms to optimize engagement.
- The strengths and challenges of paid ads versus organic strategies.
- How to design campaigns that inspire clicks, likes, and conversions by understanding audience behavior.
- Wendy's approach to social media strategy and how humor and boldness can build a relatable brand voice.

Every impactful marketing campaign begins with a deep understanding of the digital landscape. Think of platforms like social media and search engines as the foundation for building connections, driving engagement, and achieving conversions. Without an informed approach, even the most creative content risks missing the mark, failing to captivate the right audience or inspire action.

A well-rounded approach guarantees that all campaign components, paid or organic, function together to produce significant outcomes. The foundational elements of successful digital marketing will be examined in this chapter, along with platform-specific strategies, the harmony between sponsored and organic reach, and the psychological cues that influence user engagement.

4.1 Getting to Know the Big Players: Social Media, Search Engines, and More

The digital marketing landscape thrives on a handful of major platforms, each offering unique opportunities to connect with your audience and achieve specific objectives. These platforms can be grouped into three categories: social media, search engines, and other key channels. Understanding their strengths and how they complement each other is critical for creating impactful campaigns.

4.1.1 Social Media Platforms

Social media has revolutionized the way brands interact with consumers. Platforms like Facebook, Instagram, TikTok, LinkedIn, and YouTube offer unparalleled opportunities for engagement, storytelling, and targeted advertising. Each platform caters to distinct demographics and behaviors, requiring tailored strategies to maximize impact. Figure 4.1 provides an overview of their unique features, key content types, and best practices.

4.1.2 Search Engines

While social media drives engagement, search engines remain the cornerstone of intent-driven marketing. Platforms like Google and Bing enable businesses to connect with consumers actively seeking solutions. By combining the strengths of social media and search engines, you can create a well-rounded strategy that drives visibility and conversions.

1. **Google Ads:** With features like audience segmentation, geotargeting, and keyword targeting, Google is the industry leader in search advertising.

   - **Perfect for:** Deterring highly motivated people and overcrowding websites with visitors in order to boost e-commerce sales.

   - **Example:** For instance, a shoe company using Google Ads' "best running shoes" ad group will be visible to consumers who are looking to buy.

2. **Search Engine Optimization (SEO):** SEO is the foundation of organic visibility. Its main goal is to improve the content and structure of websites so they appear higher in search results. The long-term advantages of SEO, like more traffic and brand credibility, are priceless, even though they take time.

   - **Perfect for:** Long-term visibility, building authority, and cost-effective lead generation.

   - **Tip:** Invest in quality content and technical optimization to outperform competitors.

4.1.3 Other Channels

While search engines and social media hold the top spot in the online arena, other platforms also contribute significantly to audience engagement and brand recognition.

- **Email Marketing:** It is one of the most powerful ways to personalize touchpoints with your customer! It helps businesses to manage leads, re-engage customers, and service targeted promotional messages directly into their inboxes. It is best for retention, personalized connections, and upselling. An example of this is a fashion brand sending exclusive discounts to loyal subscribers.

- **Display Networks:** Display ads use banners, videos, and text across various websites to maintain visibility and reinforce branding. Google Display Network is a popular choice for businesses seeking broad reach. It is optimal for retargeting, raising awareness, and multi-channel campaigns. An example of this is a user browsing an online store might later encounter a banner ad for the same product while reading a blog.

- **E-commerce Platforms:** Websites like Shopify, Etsy, and Amazon facilitate product sales and offer in-app promotions. In a congested market, paid advertisements, product placement, and well-crafted product descriptions help brands stand out. It is best for reaching out to consumers directly, specializing in items, and reaching out to markets. An example of this is when a skincare brand promotes its product through Amazon Sponsored Ads to increase discoverability.

4.1.4 Why Understanding the Big Players Matters

Although each of the platforms has unique advantages, combining them well gives you a strong plan. For instance:

- Social media is adept at engaging users and narrating stories.
- Search engines bring in more than just easy visitors.
- Leads are qualified and converted by display ads and email marketing.

Strategic usage of these platforms creates a consistent web of digital marketing that gives customers access to the companies they trust at the appropriate moment.

Exercise 4.1: Platform Evaluation

You are tasked with analyzing IKEA's digital strategy. Choose **three platforms** IKEA could use to achieve specific marketing objectives. For each platform:

1. *Define the primary audience using the platform.*
2. *Identify content types that perform well on the platform.*
3. *Explain why this platform fits IKEA's business objectives.*

4.2 Creating Platform-Tailored Content

Producing content with a generic approach is not just ineffective; it also represents a missed chance. Every platform has its own unique advantages, target audiences, cultural subtleties, and technical specifications. Content that thrives on one platform may not connect with users on another because of variations in user behavior, expectations, and ways of engaging.

4.2.1. Why Tailored Content Matters

Creating tailored content is essential for maximizing engagement on digital platforms. Each platform attracts unique audiences with specific behaviors, expectations, and ways of interacting with content. For instance, LinkedIn users expect professional and insightful posts, while TikTok audiences crave entertainment and creativity. Overlooking these differences can result in content that feels out of place or irrelevant, diminishing its impact.

Tailoring your content ensures that your message resonates authentically. It aligns your brand with the culture and technical nuances of each platform, fostering a deeper connection with your audience. For an overview of what works best on popular platforms, refer to Figure 4.1.

4.2.2. Key Principles for Creating Platform-Tailored Content

1. **Understanding Platform Algorithms**

   Algorithms dictate how and where your content appears. Here's how you can maximize visibility on the various platforms:

- **Google Search and YouTube:** Focus on relevance and keyword optimization. To rank higher in search results, ensure your content aligns with specific queries or phrases that your audience is searching for. Use tools like Google Keyword Planner to identify trending terms and create videos or content that directly answer these queries.

- **Instagram and Facebook:** Engagement is key. Posts that generate likes, shares, comments, or other interactions tend to get more visibility. To achieve this, use strong visuals and add interactive features like polls, quizzes, or question stickers. Regularly analyze which posts resonate most and refine your strategy accordingly.

- **Twitter:** Timeliness drives success. Post regularly, and stay engaged with trending topics or hashtags relevant to your brand. Quick, thoughtful responses to ongoing conversations can amplify your reach and position you as an active participant in your industry.

- **TikTok:** Let your creativity and consistency shine. The platform's algorithm rewards videos that grab attention quickly and encourage replays or shares. Use trending audio, participate in challenges, and post regularly to keep your content fresh and visible.

2. **Choosing the Right Content Type for the Platform**

- **Static Posts (Images or Text):** These are perfect for platforms like Instagram, LinkedIn, and Facebook, where users engage with visually compelling or informative posts. An example is an Instagram product presentation with eye-catching images and a memorable caption.

- **Short-Form Videos:** TikTok, YouTube Shorts, and Instagram Reels are excellent platforms for presenting brief, interesting material. Quick product demos, trends, or relatable humor work well.

- **Long-Form Content:** For audiences seeking depth, YouTube videos, LinkedIn articles, and blog posts offer storytelling opportunities. Tutorials, interviews, or case studies are ideal for these platforms.

4.2.3. Best Practices for Popular Platforms

Different social media platforms attract unique audiences with specific expectations, offering distinct opportunities for advertisers. By understanding what works best on each platform, you can customize your content to maximize impact. Figure 4.1 highlights these differences, showcasing audience expectations, key content types, and examples.

Figure 4.1	BEST PRACTICES FOR POPULAR PLATFORMS

	Instagram	TikTok	LinkedIn	YouTube
Audience Expectation	Aesthetic visuals, Aspirational content, Interactive features	Authenticity Humor Trend-based creativity	Professionalism Thought leadership	High-quality video content offering value or entertainment
Key Content Types	Carousel posts Stories Reels User-generated content (UGC)	Challenges Lip-syncing Short tutorials Behind-the-scenes content	Case studies Industry insights Company culture highlights	Tutorials Product reviews Vlogs
Example	A travel brand could use Stories to share daily trip itineraries, while Reels might highlight scenic destinations.	A sustainable beauty brand could create Tik Toks demonstrating quick skincare routines using their products.	A software company could publish a post detailing how their product improved efficiency for a specific client.	A fitness brand might create workout tutorials featuring their equipment.

4.2.4 Example: Starbucks' Seasonal Campaigns

Starbucks is great at producing content specifically for Instagram, a platform where images capture attention. For their seasonal beverages, like the Pumpkin Spice Latte, they design eye-catching posts with beautiful backgrounds, detailed shots of the drinks, and captions that resonate with their audience.

- They leverage hashtags like #PSL and partner with influencers to spread the campaign further.
- Starbucks also encourages user-generated content (e.g., customers sharing their seasonal drink photos), boosting engagement and reach organically.

This approach works because it aligns perfectly with Instagram's visual and aspirational culture while keeping the content shareable and on-trend as illustrated in Figure 4.2.

Figure 4.2 **STARBUCKS' SEASONAL CAMPAIGN**

Source: (Instagram: @Starbucks)

Exercise 4.2: Content Creation

Imagine creating a TikTok advertisement for any brand. You must produce content that is interesting, genuine, and relatable while still being tailored to TikTok's creative culture and speed. Your tech-savvy audience enjoys humorous, relatable, concise, and memorable images. Use this framework:

1. **The Hook (First 3 Seconds):** *Craft an opening that grabs attention immediately*

2. **Visual Appeal:** *Incorporate dynamic transitions, trendy effects, text overlays, or music to amplify the message.*

3. **Highlight Value:** *Showcase the product or message in a way that connects with the audience's values*

4. **Call to Action (CTA):** *End with a clear, engaging prompt for viewers to take action*

4.3 Paid Ads vs. Organic Reach

Paid advertisements and organic reach are key components in digital marketing. These increase brand awareness, encourage interaction, and increase transactions. Every technique has a specific function, and the secret to a successful campaign is understanding how to balance various tactics.

4.3.1. Organic Reach: Slow and Steady Growth

Organic reach is about cultivating trust and building a loyal audience through consistent and authentic engagement. This strategy focuses on connecting with users without direct monetary investment, but its impact requires time and dedication.

- **Key Benefits:** Organic reach fosters credibility and builds relationships over time. Brands that use organic strategies effectively often have more authentic and meaningful interactions with their audience. Additionally, content such as blogs, SEO, and social media posts can continue driving traffic long after being published, offering sustainable growth.

- **Challenges to Consider:** Although organic reach is a less expensive option, content visibility to followers may be limited by the ever-changing algorithms on social media sites like Facebook and Instagram. Growth may therefore be slow, and it may take a lot of time and effort to make progress in a competitive setting.

4.3.2. Paid Ads: Accelerating Visibility

Through paid advertising, marketers may virtually instantly reach a wider, more focused audience and get over algorithmic limitations. Strong audience segmentation options are available on platforms like Google Ads, Instagram, Facebook, and TikTok, allowing marketers to focus on particular demographics, interests, and geographic areas.

- **Key Benefits:** Paid advertising is the ideal option for campaigns that need results immediately (think of time-sensitive goals like product launches or seasonal promotions). This is because they function immediately as paid advertisements. Additionally, they make it possible for enhanced targeting and retargeting to send brands to the appropriate audience at the appropriate moment.

- **Challenges to Manage:** Paid campaigns require careful planning and budget management. Without a proper strategy, poorly executed ads can result in wasted spending and low ROI. Additionally, reliance on paid ads without building organic credibility can make a brand seem less authentic.

4.3.3. Integrating Paid and Organic Strategies

Paid ads and organic reach are complementary approaches that, when combined effectively, can amplify your brand's impact. Paid advertising delivers immediate visibility, while organic strategies build long-term trust and loyalty. Together, they create a balanced, dynamic approach that evolves based on performance and audience behavior.

As illustrated in Figure 4.3, the integration process begins with 'Develop a Combined Strategy,' which establishes a unified goal for both approaches. For example, organic content can drive awareness and engagement, while paid ads re-target users who showed interest but didn't convert. By leveraging analytics, you can track how each strategy supports the other and adjust your efforts for optimal results.

Figure 4.3 HOW TO INTEGRATE PAID AND ORGANIC STRATEGIES

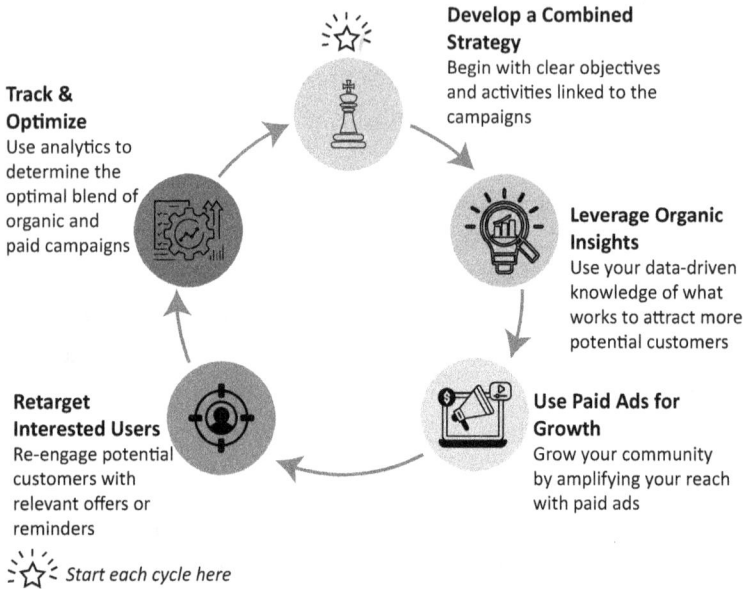

Develop a Combined Strategy
Begin with clear objectives and activities linked to the campaigns

Leverage Organic Insights
Use your data-driven knowledge of what works to attract more potential customers

Use Paid Ads for Growth
Grow your community by amplifying your reach with paid ads

Retarget Interested Users
Re-engage potential customers with relevant offers or reminders

Track & Optimize
Use analytics to determine the optimal blend of organic and paid campaigns

Start each cycle here

4.3.4 Example: Glossier

Glossier, a beauty brand known for its millennial and Gen Z appeal, exemplifies this integrated approach:

- **Organic:** Glossier uses its Instagram page to share user-generated content, tutorials, and community stories, building an authentic connection with followers.

- **Paid Ads:** The brand complements its organic efforts with paid Instagram and Google ads, focusing on product launches or special promotions. These ads often highlight their best-selling items while linking back to the organic posts that feature real customer reviews.

- **Result:** The organic content strengthens trust and authenticity, while paid ads ensure visibility among new audiences.

Exercise 4.3: Strategic Budget Allocation

You have a $10,000 marketing budget to allocate on paid and organic for an e-commerce brand focused on sustainable outdoor products for millennials (ages 18–35) and Gen-Z target audiences that are extremely proficient in the use of social platforms like YouTube, Pinterest, Instagram, and TikTok.

Key Considerations:

- **Short-term Goals:** *Drive traffic to the website and increase sales during a seasonal promotion.*

- **Long-term Goals:** *Build brand trust, authority, and community through educational content.*

- **Target Audience:** *Active on social media, responsive to visually engaging and purpose-driven content.*

Deliverables:

1. *Provide a written plan that breaks down the $10,000 budget with percentages or exact dollar amounts allocated to each strategy.*

2. *Justify your allocations, emphasizing the alignment with the business's goals.*

3. *Provide suggestions for measuring success and rebalancing the budget based on performance metrics.*

4.4 What Makes People Engage?

At its core, engagement stems from understanding human psychology. People connect with content that strikes an emotional chord, addresses a challenge, or aligns with their personal beliefs. Effective brands leverage these motivations by producing content that appears relevant, significant, and practical.

Engagement shows how strongly your content connects with the audience and goes beyond likes or comments. High engagement signals to platform algorithms that your content is valuable, leading to greater visibility. For brands, this creates a ripple effect, driving awareness, trust, and ultimately, conversions.

4.4.1. Key Triggers of Engagement

- **Emotional Resonance:** Highly emotive content (humor, nostalgia, inspiration, empathy) tends to be engaging and keep viewers watching for longer. People are more likely to act, share, or comment when these types of feelings are there. For example, a campaign showcasing heartfelt customer stories or light-hearted memes relevant to a target audience can boost shares and reactions.

- **Clear and Actionable CTAs:** Engagement increases when users know exactly what to do next. The content in the user's hand has obvious engagement routes established by phrases like "Swipe Up," "Download Now," or "Learn More." The simplicity of a call-to-action can significantly influence the number of people who click through.

- **Fear of Missing Out (FOMO):** People are naturally drawn to exclusivity and urgency. Limited-time deals, early-bird offers, or access to "members-only" content can compel users to act quickly out of fear that they'll miss a unique opportunity. For instance, brands promoting flash sales or countdown timers for an event see higher engagement due to this psychological trigger.

- **Personalization:** Customizing content to reflect individual preferences or behaviors creates a sense of connection and relevance. When individuals recognize themselves in the content, they are more inclined to engage with it. For example, Spotify Wrapped offers users customized playlists and insights, generating significant interaction by honoring personal uniqueness while tapping into nostalgia and pride.

Exercise 4.4: Crafting Engaging Content

Create a social media post designed to maximize engagement for a brand of your choice.

a. *Choose a specific emotion or psychological trigger to target (e.g., humor or FOMO).*

b. *Make a compelling call-to-action for your brand.*

c. *Explain why your approach would resonate with the intended audience and why it would reach the decision-making platform.*

In Conclusion

To increase engagement and boost conversions, it is essential to acknowledge the importance of the digital ecosystem. Understanding important channels like social media and search engines will help you create content that appeals to a range of users. Reach is increased, and sustained growth is encouraged by finding a balance between paid and organic advertising.

In addition, understanding what actually motivates participation, be it interactive features, emotional resonance, or FOMO, guarantees that your campaigns create lasting relationships. In order to turn clicks and likes into lasting relationships and observable results, success ultimately requires a smooth mix of strategy, creativity, and human understanding.

Chapter Summary

- Digital marketing relies heavily on e-commerce platforms, social media, and search engines.

- Tailored content increases engagement by aligning with platform-specific features and audience expectations.

- Paid ads provide instant visibility, while organic reach builds long-term trust.

- Psychological triggers like FOMO and emotional appeals drive user engagement.

- A clear digital ad plan ensures campaigns are targeted, measurable, and aligned with business goals.

Quiz

1. In B2B marketing, what platform takes the top spot?
   a. Snapchat
   b. Instagram
   c. LinkedIn
   d. TikTok

2. What does PPC stand for?
   a. Pay-Per-Click
   b. People Per Click
   c. Promote Paid Content
   d. Paid Platform Content

3. The main goal of SEO in digital marketing, what is it?
   a. Creating viral videos
   b. Running email campaigns
   c. Generating paid ads
   d. Increasing organic search visibility

4. What's that metric called that tracks the share of site visitors ticking off a must-do action?
   a. Bounce rate
   b. Conversion rate
   c. Click-through rate (CTR)
   d. Engagement rate

5. **What is the maximum character limit for a tweet on Twitter (now X)?**
   a. 140
   b. 280
   c. 320
   d. 200

6. **Select what they mean by a "call-to-action" (CTA):**
   a. A type of advertisement targeting conversions
   b. A list of social media hashtags
   c. A promotional discount code
   d. A button or text encouraging users to take action

7. **What is the primary audience for Pinterest?**
   a. Business executives
   b. Millennials and Gen Z, predominantly women
   c. Older adults over 50
   d. Gamers and tech enthusiasts

8. **What does CTR stand for?**
   a. Conversion Target Reach
   b. Cost-to-Ratio
   c. Click-Through Rate
   d. Content Traffic Relevance

9. **Which of the following is a long-form content format?**
   a. Blog post
   b. Instagram story
   c. Twitter post
   d. Facebook comment

10. **Which platforms are best for short-form videos?**
    a. YouTube Shorts and TikTok
    b. LinkedIn and Pinterest
    c. Facebook and Snapchat
    d. Google Ads and Bing

Answers

1 – c	2 – a	3 – d	4 – b	5 – b
6 – d	7 – b	8 – c	9 – a	10 – a

Case Study: Wendy's Social Media Strategy

Fast-food companies' advertising strategies have changed as a result of Wendy's bold and humorous social media strategy. By using this technique, Wendy's hopes to attract younger customers, increase in-person and online conversation, and appear more authentic.

GOALS

- **Relatability:** Wendy's stands apart from the usual rigid company attitude thanks to its witty and quick vibe, which appeals to the younger audience.

- **Engaging Gen Z and Millennials:** Wendy's uses humorous and interactive advertisements to draw in tech-savvy young adults. They appreciate Wendy's authenticity and new ideas.

- **Driving Sales:** Beyond engagement, Wendy's strategically links online buzz to in-store promotions, ensuring tangible business outcomes.

STRATEGIES

- **Twitter Roasts:** Wendy's witty, snarky replies on Twitter consistently go viral, generating millions of impressions and reinforcing its bold brand voice.

- **Viral Trends:** By participating in popular memes and debates, Wendy's keeps its content fresh and culturally relevant, ensuring it remains top of mind for its audience.

- **Interactive Campaigns:** The annual National Roast Day invites users to engage directly with the brand, fostering community and increasing visibility.

RESULTS

Wendy's strategy scored some real wins. They racked up a 15% jump in their Twitter following in just 12 months, plus sales went up by 10% when they threw shade on National Roast Day. These numbers show just how much they punch the right kind of real-talk and culture-savvy marketing packs.

WHY IT'S A HIT

The Real Deal

Wendy's did more than just continue with their corporate yawn fests. People took notice when they became bold and humorous. The younger demographic, who enjoy businesses that don't just talk at them but stay true to themselves, responds well to that sincere vibe.

Cultural Relevance

They use current trends and memes to stay up to date. In this manner, they are constantly present in the online conversation that their supporters are already a part of. In order to keep things interesting, relevant, and up-to-date with current trends, Wendy's isn't hesitant to make jokes about its competitors or join a heated online debate.

Two-Way Interaction

By interacting directly with consumers, the brand fosters conversation rather than a monologue. Instead of being merely passive recipients of the brand's messaging, this encourages a feeling of community and connection where customers feel engaged with the brand's identity and voice.

Watch the following video for a compilation of Wendy's Roasts on social media through our online resources.

Source: McCall, 2022

Exercise: Build Your Digital Ad Plan

Promoting a new range of environmentally friendly skincare products is part of your job as Director of the GlowBar marketing team. The campaign's objective is to draw in Gen Z and Millennial customers who are enthusiastic about environmental sustainability. The main goal of GlowBar is to promote eco-friendly glamour while offering the greatest pure skincare products.

Develop a comprehensive digital ad plan covering the following:

1. *Identify the target audience.*
2. *Choose three platforms and justify your selection*
3. *Create a sample ad for one platform*
4. *Define success metrics (e.g., engagement rate, ROI).*

Further Learning

Links also available in Online Resources:

Wendy's roasts on social media
http://bit.ly/4m8wRjy

CHAPTER 5

Crafting Ads that Sell and Stick

Key Learning Objectives

- How to craft captivating headlines that draw in readers' interest
- The psychological impact of color on the feelings and actions of viewers
- How storytelling is used in making your advertisement memorable and approachable
- Tested layout techniques that increase clicks and focus attention
- Case studies that showcase how small tweaks can deliver big results

Have you ever stopped scrolling just because an ad caught your eye? Can you remember what caught your attention? The headline? The color? The layout? Great ads are deliberately designed to capture the audience's interest, evoke strong feelings, and motivate action. They don't just happen.

The psychology of an effective message, the impact of layout and color on the user's thinking, and how to write an attention-grabbing headline that stops people from scrolling are all covered in this chapter, which will help you better comprehend the world of great advertisements.

5.1 Headlines that Stop the Scroll

People are known to peruse the internet rapidly. Thus, a catchy headline is essential to drawing in readers. Whether your advertisement is seen or disregarded is often determined by it. Not only is a compelling headline an introduction, but it is also the decisive factor that draws in readers.

To stand out, your headline must do three critical things: instantly grab attention, spark curiosity or emotion, and compel the audience to keep reading or take action.

5.1.1 Characteristics of a Winning Headline

Clarity, curiosity, emotion, and urgency are all components that make a headline stand out and instantly capture attention. These characteristics also cater to mental cues that guide decisions and drive engagement.

Applying these headline techniques will increase click-through rates, improve engagement, and ensure that your advertisements have a significant impact on your audience. Figure 5.1 below outlines four essential characteristics of a successful headline and is followed by examples and analysis of their effectiveness.

| Figure 5.1 | CHARACTERISTICS OF A WINNING HEADLINE |

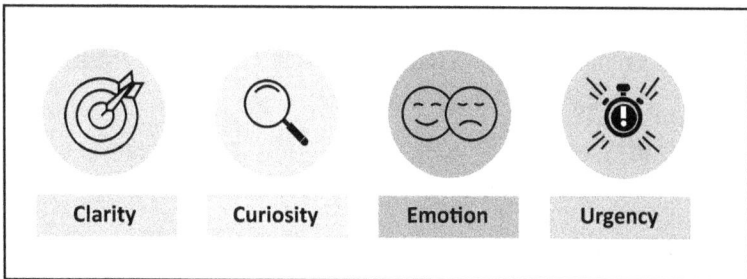

Clarity   Curiosity   Emotion   Urgency

1. **Clarity:** Your title should emphasize a distinct benefit and get right to the point. Concentrate on making a particular promise because an uninformed audience won't pay attention.

   - **Example:** "Save 50% on flights to Europe this weekend!"
   - **Why it works:** It is straightforward, provides an instant advantage, and outlines a timeline.

2. **Curiosity:** People are motivated by curiosity to find solutions, which increases the likelihood that they will click or continue reading. Grab readers' attention with a mystery, query, or startling claim.

   - **Example:** "Flawless skin? This is something dermatologists swear by."
   - **Why it works:** It raises a question that the audience wants answered, positioning your content as the solution.

3. **Emotion:** Audiences are particularly moved by headlines that appeal to their desires, anxieties, or goals. Reader engagement is higher when they feel understood.

   - **Example:** "Stop Losing Sales: A Guide to Double Your Revenue in 30 Days."
   - **Why it works:** It addresses a pain issue (losing sales) and promises a revolutionary outcome.

4. **Urgency:** Special offers or limited-time promotions are especially effective.

   - **Example:** "24 Hours to Claim Your Discount!"
   - **Why it works:** The countdown encourages readers to act immediately rather than defer doing so.

Exercise 5.1: Write Your Own Winning Headlines

Choose a product or service and craft three headlines:

1. **Focus on Clarity:** Clearly state a benefit or result.
2. **Evoke Curiosity:** Pose a question or hint at a surprising outcome.
3. **Create Urgency:** Use time-sensitive language to drive immediate action.

5.1.2 Pro tips for headline success

The best headlines incorporate a number of essential elements: they are tailored to the target audience, express their promise succinctly, and are refined by testing and analysis. For example, a succinct title that emphasizes benefits, like "Lose 10 Pounds in 30 Days—Guaranteed!" can be improved by experimenting with versions like:

1. *"Want to drop ten pounds in a month? This is Your Guide!"*
2. *"The Weight Loss Challenge That Has Everyone Talking"*

Here are some pointers to create such headlines:

1. **Test Different Headlines:** Test them out and see which one your audience likes. For A/B testing, use Ads Manager and Google Ads; if you have specific requirements, use Optimizely. Show your audience different headlines and track engagement, conversion rates, and CTR. Testing will help get better returns on investment by making data-driven decisions.

2. **Align With Your Audience:** Tailoring your message makes it relevant and creates a stronger emotional connection, which drives more engagement.

   - **Tips for alignment:** Use language and style your audience relates to. For example:
     - A playful headline like "Crush Your Fitness Goals with These Fun Workouts!" works for a younger, active audience.
     - A professional headline like "Streamline Your Business Operations with AI-Powered Tools" is for corporate decision-makers.
     - Make reference to the goals or problems of the audience.

3. **Look At High Performing Headlines:** Success leaves clues. Study top-performing campaigns in your industry or from competitors, and you'll find patterns, trends, and winning formulas to use for your own headlines. Learning what works speeds up the process of writing great headlines.

- **How to use this:**
  - Analyze competitor ads, email subject lines, or social media posts with high engagement.
  - Find the common themes, e.g., benefit-focused phrases, questions, or urgency cues.

4. **Keep It Short and Snappy:** Short attention spans and long headlines will lose your audience before they even start reading. A short, to-the-point headline gets the message across. Headlines between 8 and 12 words work best.

- **How to simplify:**
  - Remove extra words. Instead of "Learn How You Can Save Money with This Limited-Time Offer," write "Save Big with This Limited-Time Offer."
  - Focus on one key benefit or idea.

Shorter headlines are easier to read, remember, and act on, especially in digital environments like social media or search ads.

By using these pro tips, you can write headlines that grab attention. Check out Neil Patel's "How to Write Headlines That Convert" in the Online Resources section to see how this is done.

Now, let's look at how stories make ads memorable and relatable, which means clicks and ultimately sales.

5.2 The Power of Storytelling in Ads

Humans are natural storytellers and listeners. We love stories. They captivate us, make information stick, and connect us emotionally. In advertising, storytelling transforms your message into an experience, making your product feel more valuable than a purchase; it becomes a solution or possibly a dream fulfilled.

Even in short-form ads where every word counts, storytelling can shine. With as few as 30 words, you can tell a story that resonates with your audience by highlighting their problem, your solution, and the transformation your product brings.

5.2.1. Why storytelling works in ads

Storytelling turns your message into more than just information. It makes it an experience that resonates, persuades, and inspires action.

Here are three reasons why storytelling is a powerful tool for ads:

1. **Emotional Connection:** Stories connect with the audience's emotions—joy, relief, or hope—making the ad unforgettable.
2. **Relevance:** When your story is like their story, they feel seen and trusted.
3. **Persuasion:** Stories lead the audience to see your product in their life and nudge them towards a purchase.

5.2.2. How to Create a 30-Word Story That Sells

A 30-word story needs focus, clarity, and a structure that works. Start by introducing a relatable problem that grabs your audience's attention and makes them wonder what's next. For example, "After days of dinner hell, I was defeated."

Once you've introduced the problem, introduce your solution as the hero of the story—something that fixes the problem. A good one would be "Then I found FreshBox. Dinner's ready in 10 minutes."

Finally, finish with a transformation that shows the benefit your product brings to your audience and helps them imagine their own better life. For example, "My family's eating healthier, and I have time to chill."

Together, these elements create a short but powerful story that connects and provokes action. Some examples of 30-word stories in ads include:

1. **Travel Service**

   - **Problem:** "I thought Europe was out of my budget."
   - **Solution:** "BudgetWander found me a $99 flight to Paris."
   - **Transformation:** "Now I'm sipping coffee at the Eiffel Tower."

2. **Fitness App**

   - **Problem:** "I couldn't stick to my workouts."
   - **Solution:** "Then I joined FitFlow. It keeps me on track with daily challenges."
   - **Transformation:** "Now I've lost 10 pounds and feel stronger every day."

3. **Online Learning Platform**

   - **Problem:** "I was stuck in my career and had no idea how to get ahead."
   - **Solution:** "SkillUp taught me coding in 3 months."

- **Transformation:** "Now I have my dream job as a web developer."

Once you've hooked your audience with a great story, the right colors can influence what happens next through the power of emotional connection. Refer to Simon Lancaster's "The Science of Storytelling" in the Online Resources section to see this in action.

Exercise 5.2: Write Your Own 30-Word Story

Here are some tips:

1. **Choose Something You Love:** Pick a product that has made a difference in your life or one you love.

2. **Follow the Formula:** Write a story that shows a customer pain point, introduces the product as the solution, and ends with a happy transformation.

3. **Make it Personal:** Authenticity is key—stories work best when they feel real.

5.3 Color Psychology: Why the Right Colors Matter

Color in ads is more than just making them look pretty. Color plays a deep role in perception, mood, and behavior. These are psychological cues that can influence how people feel about your brand and its activities. You can influence people's perceptions of your brand and their next course of action by selecting the right colors for your advertisements.

For example, the right color can make your call-to-action buttons irresistible, make them trust your brand, or convey luxury without you having to say luxury. Effective use of color psychology means every design decision contributes to the message and emotional impact of your ad.

5.3.1. How Colors Shape Advertising

Each color has its own psychological value and can set the tone for your ad. Table 5.1 below provides a summary of the top five colors used in advertising: their meaning, how to use them, and where they can be applied effectively.

Table 5.1   TOP FIVE COLORS USED IN ADVERTISING

Color	Icon	What It Symbolizes	How to use it	Where to use it
RED	⚡	Passion, urgency, excitement	Drive urgency or draw attention to CTAS	Sales, limited-time offers, food ads
BLUE	🛡	Trust, reliability, calm	Build credibility and foster a sense of trust	Financial services, healthcare, tech
YELLOW	💡	Optimism, happiness, creativity	Grab attention and evoke energy	Ads targeting kids, creative brands
GREEN	🤲	Health, nature, sustainability	Promote eco-friendliness or wellbeing	Environmentally-conscious brands, wellness products
BLACK	💎	Sophistication, luxury, authority	Highlight exclusivity and premium appeal	Luxury branding, fashion, upscale products

Let's take an example of how to bring color to life in advertising. Imagine you're creating an ad for a fitness app. You want health fanatics to download your app and commit to a healthier life. To do that, you could use green to mean energy, vitality, and growth and link the app to health and progress. To add urgency, you could add a bold red CTA button with *"Start Your Free Trial Today!"* Green attracts and reassures; red drives action.

5.3.2. Enhancing Ads with Strategic Color Choices

To get the most out of color psychology, align your choices with your brand and your target audience. Consistency is key – your ads should match your logo, website, and packaging to build recognition and trust. Similarly, your colors should match the tone of your message.

For instance, a light-hearted advertisement for a children's toy might emphasize blues and yellows. To feel opulent, an advertisement for a high-end watch line might heavily feature black and metallic hues.

5.3.3. Balance Creativity with Functionality

While color can evoke emotions, readability and accessibility should never be sacrificed. Choose combinations that make your message stand out and look good on all devices. The best colors are the ones that feel true to your brand and its story, and the art and science of color.

With a considered approach to color psychology, your ads will grab attention, build trust, evoke emotion and action, and stay with your audience. Refer to Hubspot's "Color Psychology in Marketing" in the Online Resources section to see how this is done.

Exercise 5.3: Color Psychology in Ads
Look at an ad from a brand you love. What are the main colors, and how do they make you feel? Then what if the colors were different?

5.4 Layouts that Work: Design Basics for Catchy Ads

The layout of an ad is a tool to direct your audience's attention and action. A good layout ensures your message is clear, visually appealing, and easy to process. A well-structured design leads the viewer's eye through your content, to the headline, imagery, and call-to-action (CTA).

At its heart, a good layout is about usability and looks. By combining looks with messaging, your ad becomes more attractive and persuasive.

An effective ad layout strategically guides your audience to absorb key information and take the desired action while looking good. Here are some practical steps to implement this.

1. **Start with a Strong Focal Point:**

    Every ad should have a clear visual hierarchy, with one dominant element to grab attention immediately. This could be a bold headline, a vibrant image, or even a high-contrast button. To achieve this:

    - Place the headline or primary visual at the top or center of the ad, as these are natural focal points for the viewer's eye.

    - Make this element larger than the others to assert its dominance. For instance, a bold "50% OFF" headline should visually outweigh the supporting text.

2. Create a Logical Flow

Guide your audience's eyes through the ad in the order you want them to process information. A typical flow looks like this:

- Step 1 - Attention-grabbing headlines that convey the benefit (Lose Weight Without Dieting) are key.
- Step 2 - Visuals (a happy, energetic person) emotionally reinforce the message.
- Step 3 - The CTA button encourages immediate action ("Start Your Free Trial").

Practical Tip: Use the "Z-pattern" layout, where the eye scans from the top left (headline) diagonally through the center (visual or supporting text) and ends at the bottom right (CTA).

3. Use Whitespace Strategically

Whitespace is not wasted. Used right, it's a powerful tool to highlight your ads' best bits. A cluttered design will overwhelm the viewer, whereas proper spacing will create focus. Here's how to do it:

- Leave space around your CTA button so it stands out.
- Don't pack too much text or imagery into one area; give your headline some room to breathe.
- Balance your elements so the viewer's eye can flow.

4. Leverage Contrast for Clarity

Contrast makes your ad stand out and ensures important info isn't missed. Here's how to use contrast:

- Use a bold, high-contrast color for your CTA button (e.g., red or orange on a white background) so it can't be ignored.
- Pair a bold headline with lighter, smaller supporting text for readability and emphasis.

- Make sure your visuals support the text, not compete with it. For instance, the eye is drawn to a bright product image on a plain background.

5. **Keep Visual and Brand Consistency**

Ad designs should mirror your brand identity so your message is instantly recognizable. This means:

- Limit your font usage to two font families. For example, a bold font for headlines and a simple, clean font for body text.
- Stick to your brand's color palette. A travel brand, for instance, might use bright blues and greens to evoke adventure and nature.
- Use high-quality, relevant images that match your brand tone—real photos for personal brands or polished visuals for luxury products.

6. **Test and Optimize**

Once your ad layout is live, it's essential to gather feedback and improve. Use heatmaps or A/B testing to identify which elements work best. For instance:

- Perform A/B Tests with the headline placement. Does the headline work better at the top or below the image?
- Adjust the contrast. Try different button colors to see which gets the most clicks.
- Simplify the layout. If viewers are bouncing quickly, reduce clutter or reposition key elements.

The key is to keep the design clean, focused, and aligned with your audience's preferences. Refer to The Futur's "Basics of Visual Design for Ads" in the Online Resources section to see how this is done.

Exercise 5.4: A Layout in Action

Create an ad for a meal subscription service using the following layout:

- *Headline*
- *Supporting Visual*
- *Body Text*
- *CTA Button*

In Conclusion

Creating ads that sell is both an art and a science. It all comes down to knowing what your audience needs, wants, and fears and meeting them where they are.

By mastering scroll-stopping headlines, compelling stories, intentional color, and strategic layout, you can create ads that grab attention and build connections. Every great ad is an invitation to your audience to engage, trust, and act.

Chapter Summary

- Colors are powerful emotional triggers that influence perceptions and actions. Red evokes urgency and excitement, blue fosters trust, and green promotes health and sustainability.

- A well-structured layout uses visual hierarchy to guide attention from the headline to the supporting visuals and ends with the CTA. Whitespace, contrast, and consistency ensure the ad is clean, compelling, and aligned with the brand identity.

- Stories connect with people. Start with a problem, introduce your product as the solution, and end with a transformation and a clear CTA to take the next step (click, sign up, buy).

- Consistency in fonts, colors, and style builds trust and brand recognition.

- Use bold headlines, great images, and colorful CTAs to grab attention.

- Testing and refining ad elements, such as A/B testing headlines and CTAs, ensures the final design resonates with the target audience.

Quiz

1. **What is the primary purpose of visual hierarchy in ad design?**
    a. To use as many fonts as possible
    b. To ensure the audience focuses on the most important elements first
    c. To add decorative elements to the ad
    d. To create a cluttered design for more impact

2. **Which of the following colors is most commonly associated with trust?**
    a. Red
    b. Yellow
    c. Blue
    d. Black

3. **What is whitespace in ad design?**
    a. The unused area between design elements
    b. A type of background color
    c. An area reserved for text only
    d. A section for adding more visual details

4. **What emotional response does the color red typically evoke in advertising?**
    a. Calm and relaxation
    b. Excitement and urgency
    c. Trust and reliability
    d. Luxury and sophistication

5. **What was the key feature of Airbnb's "Made Possible by Hosts" campaign?**

   a. Offering discounts on bookings
   b. Sharing real-life stories of hosts and travelers
   c. Highlighting the technical features of the app
   d. Encouraging group travel experiences

6. **Which of the following best describes contrast in ad design?**

   a. The use of similar colors to create harmony
   b. Using the same font size throughout the design
   c. Adding multiple patterns to the background
   d. Highlighting differences between elements to draw attention

7. **How many words should a headline typically have for maximum impact?**

   a. 3-5
   b. 8-12
   c. 15-20
   d. 20+

8. **In storytelling for ads, what should come after highlighting the problem?**

   a. Introducing your solution
   b. Asking for feedback
   c. Adding a secondary headline
   d. Including a discount offer

9. Why is consistency important in ad design?
   a. It allows for more variety in styles.
   b. It reinforces your brand identity.
   c. It makes the ad appear more complex.
   d. It ensures all design elements are bold.

10. What is the purpose of the CTA (Call-to-Action) in an ad?
    a. To display the brand's logo
    b. To add decorative text
    c. To summarize the content of the ad
    d. To direct viewers toward a specific action

Answers

1 – b	2 – c	3 – a	4 – b	5 – b
6 – d	7 – b	8 – a	9 – b	10 – d

Case Study 1: Old Spice: The Man Your Man Could Smell Like (2010)

Old Spice was a brand associated with an older demographic and needed to reinvent itself for a younger audience. Enter the 2010 campaign "The Man Your Man Could Smell Like," a bold, funny, and unforgettable approach that became a cultural phenomenon.

Key Strategies:

- **Humor as a Hook:** The campaign had an over-the-top character – a smooth, confident, and charming guy, delivering ridiculous one-liners directly to the camera. Humor wasn't random; it was designed to appeal to both men (the primary user) and women (the purchaser).

- **Scarcity & Urgency:** Old Spice tapped into the idea of scarcity by making the product the key to being "the man your man could smell like." This created an emotional urgency for women to buy the product for their men.

- **Emotional Appeal:** Beyond humor, the campaign struck an emotional chord by connecting with insecurities and aspirations. For men, it promised confidence and desirability; for women, it offered the fantasy of the "perfect man."

- **Viral, Shareable Content:** The campaign leveraged platforms like YouTube, where its quirky videos quickly went viral. Old Spice even responded to fan comments with personalized video replies, fostering engagement and a sense of community.

Impact:

These strategies brought Old Spice body wash sales up 125% in 6 months. This proved that you can make old products new again with bold creativity and humor.

Source: (SmithBrothersmedia, 2021)

Case Study 2: Airbnb: Made Possible by Hosts (2021)

The "Made Possible by Hosts" campaign from Airbnb in 2021 was perfectly timed. The world had changed because of the COVID-19 pandemic, and trust between hosts and guests was a major issue. Airbnb wanted to re-establish trust and reiterate its founding principles of connection and community.

Key Strategies:

- **Storytelling Through Real Experiences:** The campaign featured real stories of hosts and travelers, showing how Airbnb created personal connections. For example, a host helping a traveler celebrate a milestone or guests staying in amazing spaces. This humanized the platform and made it relatable and trustworthy.

- **Emotional Connection:** By using real-life stories, Airbnb triggered emotions like nostalgia, gratitude, and warmth. These stories reminded people of the joy of travel and the role of human connection in making experiences special.

- **Community-Focused Messaging:** The campaign promoted the platform and celebrated the hosts who made it possible. By centering the hosts in the narrative, Airbnb strengthened its image as a company built on trust, shared experiences, and mutual support.

- **Reinforcing Brand Values:** Airbnb highlighted its unique selling point: staying in homes, not hotels. This differentiated it from the competition and appealed to travelers looking for authentic experiences.

Impact:

People were searching for meaningful and safe ways to travel after the pandemic, so it worked perfectly. It rebuilt trust in Airbnb and a sense of community, which kept the brand ahead of the travel pack.

Source: Worthen, 2022

Exercise: Ad Redesign Challenge

Choose an ad you find ineffective. Improve it by:

- *Write a more engaging headline.*
- *Adding a 30-word story.*
- *Proposing a color scheme to better evoke emotions.*
- *Adjusting the layout for better clarity and engagement.*

Further Learning

Links also available in Online Resources:

1. **"How to Write Headlines That Convert" by Neil Patel**
   http://bit.ly/458ITTj
2. **"The Science of Storytelling" by Simon Lancaster**
   http://bit.ly/4miph69
3. **"Color Psychology in Marketing" by HubSpot**
   http://bit.ly/3U3MZqO
4. **"Basics of Visual Design for Ads" by The Future**
   http://bit.ly/3UmYKc5

CHAPTER 6

Brand DNA: Building Identity Through Advertising

Key Learning Objectives

- Why consistency is the key to trust and recognition in advertising.
- How to use colors, fonts, and layouts to define your brand's visual identity and emotions.
- How to craft a brand voice that speaks to your target audience.
- How to keep your brand fresh and relevant in a changing cultural and market landscape.
- Examples from real life to apply to your brand.

At the heart of every great brand is its Brand DNA – a mix of elements that define it, communicate its values, and create an emotional connection with its audience. Advertising is the vehicle to amplify and reinforce this DNA so customers perceive and remember your brand.

Building and maintaining a strong Brand DNA is all about balance: consistency and adaptability, compelling visuals and resonant messaging, and keeping your brand relevant in a changing world. From choosing the right colors and fonts to creating a brand voice and refreshing your identity over time, this chapter will show you how to align every part of your advertising strategy with your brand's core.

6.1 The Power of Consistency

The unifying factor that gives a brand its cohesive identity and appeal is consistency. You become instantly recognizable when you use the same words, tone, and images throughout all of your interactions. That feeling of familiarity strengthens your values, fosters trust, and positions you as your customers' first choice.

6.1.1 Why Consistency Matters

Consistency is a necessary aspect of any brand. Let us look at some of the reasons why it is so important:

1. **Recognition Across Channels:** Repetition is key to recognition. Your audience will associate specific visuals and messages with your brand. A consistent look and feel across digital and physical platforms means customers can spot your brand in a crowded market. For example, Coca-Cola's red and white branding, script logo, and contour bottle are recognizable everywhere, whether in a Tokyo vending machine or a New York Facebook ad.

2. **Trust-Building:** Consistency signals reliability. When your brand looks, sounds, and feels the same at every touchpoint, it tells customers you are dependable and professional. This psychological reassurance builds trust and fosters repeat business. For example, Nike's consistent use of its "Just Do It" slogan, bold visuals of

athletes, and clean typeface reassures customers they're engaging with an inspiring and high-performing brand.

3. **Reinforcing Brand Values:** Your mission and values can be communicated in every interaction with your brand. It reinforces who you are and what you stand for if your packaging, customer service, and advertising all reflect your core identity. For instance, Patagonia consistently ties its branding to sustainability. Their advertising, product tags, and website all emphasize environmental responsibility, strengthening their identity as a company committed to eco-consciousness.

6.1.2 How to Maintain Consistency as Your Brand Grows

Consistency is necessary to make sure that the identity, values, and message of your brand are consistent at every touchpoint as it expands. This builds audience trust in addition to establishing brand recognition. Below is how to achieve this:

1. **Build a Clear Brand Style Guide:** A style guide is essential for maintaining consistency across platforms. It should include:

   - Your logo and acceptable variations
   - Color codes and primary/secondary palettes
   - Approved typography styles and sizes
   - Guidelines for imagery and photography style
   - Tone of voice and messaging examples

   For example, Spotify's style guide specifies everything from color gradients to the spacing between text and images, ensuring that its sleek, modern identity stays consistent across all campaigns.

2. **Standardize Processes Across Teams:** As your company grows, multiple teams (marketing, design, social media) will contribute to your branding. Establish shared workflows and communication tools to keep everyone aligned.

3. **Use Branding Tools:** Leverage design platforms like Canva for templated content or tools like Frontify and Brandfolder to centralize and manage your assets. These platforms ensure that everyone in your organization has access to the latest approved materials.

4. **Audit Regularly:** As brands change, so does how consumers view them. To make sure your branding continues to reflect your objectives, core values, and current market trends, conduct audits every six months.

6.2 How Colors, Fonts, and Layouts Shape Identity

Your visual identity is a design choice and a powerful tool that affects how your audience sees, connects with, and remembers your business. All your design decisions, colors, fonts, and layouts add up to a beautiful brand. Let's get into how you can use it all to be you.

Visual branding is the silent language your brand speaks to your audience. Each visual component conveys emotions, values, and messages that can either attract or repel potential customers. When thoughtfully combined, colors, fonts, and layouts create a memorable identity that resonates across all touchpoints.

6.2.1. How to Choose the Right Colors

Within 90 seconds of viewing a product, consumers form opinions about it, with color accounting for 62% to 90% of these decisions (Colorcom, n.d.). Color is a big business in shaping brand perception and buying decisions. As we learned in Chapter 5:

- Choose colors that match your brand's mission and tone. For example, an eco brand might use greens and browns.
- Understand your audience. Bright colours like red or yellow are for younger, more adventurous audiences, while muted tones might be for older, more professional demographics.
- Consider cultural differences. Colors can have different meanings across cultures. For example, white means purity in Western cultures but mourning in Eastern cultures.

6.2.2. Fonts: Conveying Tone Through Typography

Typography is another key part of visual branding. Fonts convey tone, personality, and even trustworthiness. Get the font wrong, and you undermine your brand.

1. **Font Types and What They Mean**
   - **Serif Fonts:** Times New Roman or Baskerville work well for luxury brands or institutions emphasizing history and prestige. They represent tradition, elegance, and authority. Gucci and Prada use these to look timeless.
   - **Sans-serif Fonts:** Helvetica or Arial, which are commonly used by tech and startup brands to

convey simplicity and innovation. Google's logo uses this font to look approachable and creative.

- **Script Fonts:** Elegant, creative, and personal. Script fonts emulate handwriting and are often used for premium or boutique brands. Coca-Cola's script font exudes warmth and nostalgia.

- **Display Fonts:** Bold, decorative, and attention-grabbing. These are ideal for headlines or brands looking to make a statement. Disney's custom font reflects its whimsical and magical essence.

Figure 6.1 below provides an illustration of these font types.

Figure 6.1 FONT TYPES

SERIF FONTS	**Brand** Times New Roman	Brand Garamond
SAN-SERIF FONTS	**Brand** Helvetica	**Brand** Arial
SCRIPT FONTS	*Brand* Brush Script	*Brand* Alex Brush
DISPLAY FONTS	**Brand** Broadway	Brand Papyrus

2. Choosing the Right Font for Your Brand

- **Match Your Brand Personality:** A playful tech startup might opt for sans-serif fonts, while a legal firm would benefit from a serif font to emphasize professionalism.

- **Ensure Readability:** No matter how stylish, your font should be legible across all platforms and sizes.

- **Consistency is Key:** Use no more than two or three complementary fonts across your branding materials to maintain consistency.

6.2.4. Layouts: Guiding Attention and Driving Engagement

As we learned in Chapter 5, a well-designed layout ensures that your brand's message is not just seen but absorbed. Layouts combine visual hierarchy, balance, and design elements to create a seamless experience for the viewer.

For example, Spotify's brand identity thrives on its neon green and black palette, symbolizing energy and modernity. The sans-serif font reflects accessibility, while its clean layouts, focused on user preferences (e.g., playlists), create a personalized feel.

Exercise 6.1: Future-Proofing Your Brand

Imagine your brand 10 years into the future and consider the following:

- *Look at their colors, fonts, and layouts.*
- *Write down how these elements make you feel or what message they send.*

6.3 Creating a Brand Voice That Resonates

A brand voice brings your brand to life so your audience can emotionally connect with it. It's how it builds trust and stands out in a crowded market. Whether casual and chatty or formal and professional, your brand voice should mirror your audience's values, language, and aspirations.

A consistent and resonant brand voice means your audience recognizes your messages across all platforms. When done right, it makes your brand memorable, builds loyalty, and encourages deeper engagement. A clear brand voice bridges the gap between a product and its audience and turns transactions into relationships.

6.3.1. Steps to Create a Brand Voice That Resonates

Understanding your target market is essential to developing a brand voice that truly resonates. Explore their pain points, aspirations, and values, and think about the tone or language they connect with: serious, playful, or motivational. For example, Wendy's has connected with their younger, tech-savvy audience by using humor and sarcasm, especially on Twitter. This has not only made them a part of the online conversation but also a meme.

Determining the personality of your brand is a further essential phase in the process. How would your brand interact with people, act, and speak if it were a person? Would they be formal or casual? Would their tone be serious, funny, empathetic, or bold? Nike, for example, has built their identity around motivation and empowerment. Their messaging is all about overcoming and going for greatness, as summed up in their famous slogan, "Just Do It."

While maintaining a brand voice, you need to adapt your messaging to the nuances of each platform. On LinkedIn, a more professional tone might work for a business audience, while on Instagram, a more conversational tone might work better. Spotify is a great example of this. On Twitter, they use humor to engage with users; on their app, they lean into personalization by creating playlists and captions that are tailored to each user.

Authenticity leads you to establish the trust of the audience, as people are drawn towards brands that appear to be honest and transparent. Your message, when it stems from your inner values and actions, provides the audience with a sense of dependability and credibility, such as Dove's "Real Beauty" ads, which encourage diversity and question conventional notions of beauty. Dove has stayed true to themselves while building a deep connection with their audience.

Finally, your brand voice should evolve with your audience and the platforms you use. Always experiment with different styles and methods, and be open to changing without losing your essence. Airbnb, for example, shifted their voice from transactional and bookings-focused to community-driven and focused on belonging and human connection in their messaging. This has helped them stay relevant in a changing world.

Exercise 6.2: Aligning Your Brand Voice

Analyze a Brand You Admire:

- **Study their messaging across platforms** *(social media, ads, website) and identify the tone they use (e.g., playful, empowering, professional).*

- **Write and Compare Samples:** *Create three sample tweets, slogans, or taglines in their voice and compare them to their actual messaging to see if they align.*
- **Develop and Test Your Brand Voice:** *Write three sample messages in your own voice for different platforms, get feedback from others, and refine your tone to ensure it reflects your brand's personality and values.*

6.4 Keeping Your Brand Fresh and Relevant

Consistency is the foundation of branding, but adaptability is what keeps your brand alive in a changing world. Brands must balance staying true to their core while the world changes culturally, technologically, and consumer behaviourally. Refreshing your brand without losing its soul will keep it relevant and connected to your audience.

Figure 6.2 outlines practical steps you can follow to ensure your brand remains fresh and relevant. These concepts are discussed in further detail below.

Figure 6.2 KEEPING YOUR BRAND FRESH

Rebrand | Use Trends | Engage | Refresh | Use Technology

6.4.1. How to Keep Your Brand Fresh

1. **Rebranding When Necessary:** Rebranding is about refining your brand to stay current. A well-thought-out rebrand will modernize your image and attract new customers without losing your existing ones.

    Example: In 2016, Instagram replaced its skeuomorphic camera icon with a gradient-based design. The new logo was modern, on trend, and appealed to younger, tech-savvy users while still being recognisable as Instagram.

2. **Trends:** Using cultural, design, and digital trends can make your brand feel current and relevant. But trends should be used thoughtfully so they align with your brand DNA.

    Example: Burger King's 2021 retro-inspired rebrand brought back its 1969 logo with a cleaner, modern twist. By using nostalgia, the brand connected with millennial audiences and showcased its commitment to quality ingredients.

3. **Engaging with Social Issues:** Purpose-driven branding creates deeper connections with your audience by showing shared values. When done authentically, engaging with social or environmental issues will make your brand more relevant and credible.

    Example: Ben & Jerry's is famous for current social movements advocating for climate change, racial justice, and LGBTQ+ rights. This reinforces the brand's progressive positioning.

4. **Refreshing Content and Campaigns:** Sometimes, staying fresh is as simple as updating your visuals, creating new campaigns, or seasonal opportunities.

Example: Coca-Cola keeps its brand current with limited edition bottle designs and seasonal campaigns like its holiday ads featuring the Coca-Cola polar bear. These updates deepen the emotional connection while keeping the core of the brand.

5. **New Technology:** You will stay ahead of the competition if you use technology like blockchain, augmented reality, or artificial intelligence.

   Example: Nike's AR app for shoe fitting combines innovation with convenience and reinforces its performance and customer focus.

Exercise 6.3: Future-Proofing Your Brand

Imagine your brand 10 years into the future and consider the following:

- *What cultural or technological trends could influence your audience's needs?*
- *How might competitors evolve, and what would set you apart?*
- *Brainstorm three ways your branding could adapt (e.g., design updates, product offerings, messaging).*

In Conclusion

A brand is both consistent and adaptable, grounded in its core but willing to evolve. Your brand can stay ahead of the curve without losing its core by embracing technology, trends, and thoughtful updates. In times of change, balance between consistency and adaptability means your brand not only survives but thrives.

Chapter Summary

- Having a consistent message and design across all platforms builds trust, recognition, and loyalty so your audience feels connected to your brand.

- Colors, fonts, and layouts shape how your brand is seen. Understanding color psychology, typography, and layout design will help you create a memorable and compelling brand.

- Your tone is your brand's personality and relationship with your audience. It should reflect their values and aspirations and be consistent across all touchpoints.

- Consistency is important, but adaptability is what will keep your brand thriving in a changing cultural and technological world. Thoughtful updates to your visuals, messaging, or campaigns will keep your brand relevant.

- Trends or supporting social issues can resonate with your audience when aligned with your brand values.

- Your Brand DNA is your roadmap to long-term success. Balancing consistency and adaptability will keep your brand relevant, memorable, and emotionally connected to your audience.

Quiz

1. **Why is consistency important in branding?**
   a. It ensures uniform messaging and identity across all platforms.
   b. It helps brands experiment with various identities.
   c. It avoids the need for brand updates.
   d. It allows brands to change their logo frequently.

2. **What is the primary benefit of adaptability in branding?**
   a. Maintaining customer loyalty
   b. Remaining relevant amidst cultural and technological changes
   c. Avoiding rebranding efforts
   d. Ensuring consistency across platforms

3. **What does Starbucks' green color symbolize?**
   a. Luxury and exclusivity
   b. Energy and passion
   c. Growth, sustainability, and renewal
   d. Adventure and exploration

4. **Why do brands introduce limited-edition products?**
   a. To test new products before a permanent launch
   b. To create urgency and exclusivity (FOMO)
   c. To replace old offerings
   d. To reduce production costs

5. What is a key feature of Starbucks' digital innovation?

   a. Seasonal cups
   b. Augmented reality experiences
   c. Personalized rewards via the mobile app
   d. Use of celebrity endorsements

6. How do seasonal campaigns help brands stay relevant?

   a. By connecting with annual traditions and current cultural trends
   b. By reducing operational costs during busy seasons
   c. By avoiding product innovation
   d. By keeping branding consistent without changes

7. What does the Starbucks mermaid logo represent?

   a. The city's tech industry roots
   b. The maritime history of Seattle
   c. Adventure and caffeine
   d. Simplicity and minimalism

8. Why is integrating trends important for branding?

   a. To copy competitors
   b. To attract a younger audience while staying authentic
   c. To redefine the brand identity completely
   d. To avoid creating timeless designs

9. Which of the following is an example of Starbucks adapting store designs?
   a. Eliminating in-store experiences
   b. Replacing seating areas with vending machines
   c. Maintaining identical designs globally
   d. Using sustainable materials and regional aesthetics

10. How does sustainability benefit a brand like Starbucks?
   a. Makes the brand less adaptable
   b. Increases the price of products
   c. Reduces marketing efforts
   d. Aligns the brand with eco-conscious consumer values

Answers

1 – a	2 – b	3 – c	4 – b	5 – c
6 – a	7 – b	8 – b	9 – d	10 – d

Case Study : Starbucks's Brand DNA Success

Brand color and logo

Starbucks' brand is built around its green color palette and mermaid logo, which represents growth, sustainability, and quality. These have remained the same throughout its journey, so the global audience knows what to expect.

- The mermaid logo references the brand's Seattle heritage, a city with a rich maritime history, and represents adventure and exploration.

- The green color palette is about the company's environmental responsibility and renewal, so the brand can be seen as sustainable. This timeless visual identity makes Starbucks a global icon and connects with customers.

Seasonal Campaigns and Limited-Edition Products

Starbucks uses exclusivity and anticipation through seasonal campaigns and limited edition products.

- The holiday cups and pumpkin spice lattes have become cultural events, driving customers to come back year after year.

- Limited-time drinks, seasonal packaging, and unique product lines (like cherry blossoms in Japan) create FOMO and make Starbucks a brand of the season. This builds deeper emotional connections and relevance.

Modernized Store Designs

Starbucks maintains its identity as a "third place" between home and work while updating its physical locations to reflect contemporary tastes.

New store designs incorporate local elements, sustainable materials, and modern design, making each store both unique and global. Some stores have eco-friendly features like solar panels or locally sourced materials to match customer demand for greener business.

By updating its store environment, Starbucks appeals to modernity without losing its warm and cozy feel.

Digital Innovation

Starbucks has used technology to improve the customer experience and stay ahead.

- The Starbucks app is for mobile ordering, personalized rewards, and contactless payments to match the modern convenience-driven customer.
- Digital innovation, like virtual gift cards and voice ordering, makes Starbucks a forward-thinking brand.
- In addition to increasing customer loyalty, this digital integration helps Starbucks stay on the cutting edge of technology.

Commitment to Sustainability

Sustainability is at the core of the brand for the eco-friendly consumer:

- Programs like ethically sourced coffee, reusable cups, and carbon-neutral goals show we care about the planet.
- By tackling big global issues like deforestation and plastic waste, we build trust and align with consumer values. So, we stay relevant to the socially conscious consumer.

Community Engagement

Starbucks is more than a coffee company as it builds meaningful relationships with communities.

- Through local programs like charity partnerships or youth employment initiatives, Starbucks is a company that gives back.
- In-store events like book readings or community discussions make it a social hub.
- By putting community first, Starbucks deepens customer loyalty and creates spaces that feel personal.

Balance of Familiarity and Innovation

Starbucks gets the balance of consistency and evolution right. Customers know and love the brand, products, and spaces. And are engaged by new product launches, store designs, and seasonal campaigns. So, it stays relevant to new and existing customers.

Key Takeaway

Starbucks shows how to balance consistency and adaptability. By staying true to its values (sustainability, quality, community) and evolving through technology, seasonal campaigns, and new products, Starbucks is a brand that's timeless and future-facing.

Source: (Roll, 2021)

Exercise: Unpacking Your Brand DNA

Choose a brand you're familiar with (e.g., a local business or a favorite global brand).

- *Examine their:*

    - Visual identity: Colors, fonts, layouts.
    - Brand voice: How they speak across platforms.
    - Consistency: Whether their message feels unified across all touchpoints.

- *Write a Summary: In one paragraph, describe the brand's DNA. Highlight what makes it strong and suggest ways it could stay fresh in the future.*

CHAPTER 7

Culture and Society: The Forces Shaping Advertising

Key Learning Objectives

- Cultural norms, values, and traditions in advertising
- Society and advertising trends
- Generational values
- How to create culturally aware advertising
- Lessons from real-world brands

When done well, advertising reflects and responds to the cultural and social environment it's in. Whether a brand is entering new markets, speaking to generational values, or staying relevant in a changing world, understanding culture and society is key to building effective advertising strategies.

Advertisers have to balance universal brand appeal with the specific needs and expectations of different audiences. Societal trends like sustainability, inclusivity, and technological advancement have a direct impact on how brands communicate their values. Misreading cultural cues or ignoring social priorities can lead to tone-deaf campaigns and brand damage, while cultural fluency and alignment can create deep emotional connections with consumers.

7.1 Understanding the Impact of Culture on Advertising

A group's shared values, beliefs, customs, and practices make up its culture, which is the foundation of its society. It affects how consumers see and react to ads. Good advertising respects and celebrates the audience's cultural reality. Bad advertising causes controversy, alienates the audience, and damages the brand by misunderstanding or ignoring cultural nuances.

As an advertiser, it is imperative to have an understanding of the culture you are targeting to produce culturally relevant work. Taking into account everything from language and symbols to customs and religious practices. Below, we look at some of the key cultural considerations for advertisers.

7.1.1 Why Considerations for Culturally Aligned Advertising Are Important

1. **Cultural Norms:** What is socially acceptable, valued, or celebrated within a group are its cultural norms. Advertising that goes against these norms can come across as tone-deaf or insensitive. On the other hand, advertising that conforms to them can create emotional connections. For example, humility and respect for elders are deeply ingrained cultural values in Japan. Advertising that promotes modesty and family harmony is popular with Japanese consumers.

2. **Symbols and Icons:** Symbols and icons are powerful in many cultures, representing heritage, beliefs, or values. Using culturally relevant symbols can be relatable, but misuse or misappropriation can be backlash. An example of a misstep is Dolce & Gabbana, a brand that faced criticism in China for using stereotypes in a campaign featuring a model struggling to eat pizza with chopsticks. This tone-deaf approach offended many and led to calls for boycotts. (Xu, 2018)

3. **Language and Humor:** Language is a cultural marker, and even small translation mistakes can kill a campaign. Humor is also cultural and doesn't translate well across regions. For example, in the UK, campaigns often use dry, sarcastic humor, which doesn't work in countries where humor is more direct or slapstick. Brands need to adapt their tone and wordplay to local language and cultural sensitivities.

4. **Religion and Tradition:** Religion dictates diet, dress code, and celebrations, so advertisers need to align their campaigns with these sacred values. Tradition also influences buying behavior or product preferences. For instance, in Muslim countries where halal is key, brands like Nestlé and KFC showcase their halal logos.

7.1.2 The Risks of Cultural Missteps

Brands that fail to consider cultural nuances risk alienating consumers, facing public backlash, and suffering reputational damage. Below are a few examples:

- **Pepsi's Kendall Jenner Ad:** While trying to align with social movements, this ad was criticized for being tone-deaf and culturally clueless. Check the Online resources to see how this was a misstep by Pepsi.

- **H&M's "Coolest Monkey in the Jungle" Incident:** A product description and message were perceived as racially insensitive, causing global outrage. Check the Online resources to see how this was a misstep by H&M.

Key Takeaways

It's important to remember that you can't advertise without understanding the cultural landscape of your audience.

- Do deep research into the cultural norms, symbols, and practices of your target market.
- Change language, humor, and imagery to fit local sensibilities.
- Make sure campaigns are inclusive, respectful, and don't stereotype.

By doing this, brands can create ads that resonate and build trust and long-term loyalty in diverse markets.

7.2 Society's Role in Shaping Ad Trends

Societal values and concerns change with economic, political, technological, and cultural shifts. Ad trends reflect this as brands try to match their messaging to what's on people's minds. Understanding and being responsive to these societal forces is key for advertisers who want to stay relevant and build real connections with consumers.

Today, audiences expect brands to take a stance on the things that matter to them, from environmental sustainability to inclusivity and social justice. Brands that do this through their ads get trust and loyalty; brands that don't take a stance on the things that matter to them or get it wrong lose their audience.

7.2.1. Key Societal Trends Shaping Advertising

Figure 7.1 below outlines some of the trends in the global community that are shaping advertising today. These relate to sustainability, non-exclusionism, social justice, a growing focus on mental wellness, and digital integration.

Figure 7.1 SOCIETAL TRENDS SHAPING ADVERTISING

| Sustainability | Inclusivity | Activism & Social Justice | Mental health awareness | Digital integration |

1. **Sustainability**

   Younger generations want brands that are environmentally sustainable, responsible, and transparent in their supply chain.

   - **Example:** Patagonia uses advertising to promote their sustainable business model. Their "Do not Buy This Jacket" campaign brought their brand in line with global standards by telling customers to buy less.
   - **Impact on Advertising:** Brands are highlighting their environmental footprint through visual storytelling, eco-friendly product innovation, and green messaging.

2. **Inclusivity**

   Nowadays, representation is the backbone of modern advertising. Brand campaigns need to take into account that society is more diverse in terms of race, gender, age, body type, and ability. In addition to increasing brand relatability, inclusive advertising breaks down stereotypes and gives marginalised groups a sense of community.

- **Example:** women of all shapes, sizes, and ethnicities were featured in Dove's "Real Beauty" campaign, which was all about body positivity. The campaign was praised for promoting self-worth and challenging traditional beauty standards.

- **Impact on Advertising:** To promote inclusion and equality through marketing, brands are casting more diverse actors and telling stories that appeal to a broader demographic.

3. **Activism and Social Justice**

   Customers expect brands to take a stance on social issues, from gender rights to racial equality and beyond. However, effective activism campaigns need to feel authentic, not contrived. Brands can increase brand loyalty by aligning with social justice movements and appealing to values-driven, ethically conscious consumers.

   - **Example:** Nike tackled police brutality and racial injustice head-on with Colin Kaepernick's "Dream Crazy" campaign. Despite the controversy, the campaign increased Nike's standing with their core audience, especially with younger, socially conscious customers.

   - **Impact on Advertising:** Brands that position their marketing around activism, stating their position on social issues, and adding purposeful messaging will gain traction and experience amazing results.

4. **Mental Health Awareness**

Mental health is talked about in society, and companies are realising the value of emotional well-being in their advertising. Audiences respond to ads that de-stigmatize mental health or promote self-care, especially post-pandemic.

- **Example:** the meditation apps *Calm* and *Headspace* have made mental health, mindfulness, and stress reduction the focus of their marketing. The brands are positioned as caring and helpful by these campaigns.

- **Impact on Advertising:** Wellness initiatives, partnerships with mental health organizations, and empathy-driven storytelling are now part of the advertising mix.

5. **Digital Integration**

With society's reliance on technology, brands are engaging with customers differently, and advertising strategies need to include digital touchpoints. Ads that are tech-driven, attention-grabbing, and go beyond traditional formats such as interactive media, augmented reality, and virtual reality are what customers expect.

- **Example:** Burger King's "Burn That Ad" campaign, for example, used augmented reality to allow customers to "burn" rival ads for a free Whopper. Tech-savvy audiences loved the campaign, which combined technology with friendly competition.

- **Impact on Advertising:** Ads are getting more immersive with interactive elements, gamification, and personalised digital content to grab attention and increase brand engagement.

7.2.2. Challenges of Societal Alignment

Aligning with societal trends is a big opportunity but also comes with risks.

- **Authenticity Concerns:** Consumers can spot insincere or opportunistic messaging. Brands need to walk the talk.
- **Polarization:** Addressing social issues can split audiences, and brands need to be prepared for backlash when taking a stand.
- **Cultural Sensitivity:** Mistakes in representation or messaging can damage reputation, as we've seen in past ad controversies.

One high-profile failure in the past few years was H&M's 2018 ad featuring a black child wearing a hooded sweatshirt, with the caption Coolest Monkey in the Jungle, which was widely condemned as ethnically and culturally insensitive, leading to boycotts, social media outrage, and declining brand equity. Brands need to ensure their communication is genuine and culturally relevant to avoid such pitfalls.

By aligning with societal trends in their campaigns, brands can stay relevant and build deeper relationships with their audience. Advertisers must:

- Keep up with changing societal values and issues.
- Show diversity, inclusion, and authenticity in their ads.
- Use digital to create immersive ad experiences.
- Be genuine when tackling sensitive social issues.

By doing so, brands will be seen as progressive, empathetic, and socially aware by their consumers.

Exercise 7.1: Society-Aligned Messaging

1. **Select a Societal Trend:** *Choose a key trend (e.g., sustainability, inclusivity).*

2. **Develop a Campaign:** *Design an ad concept that addresses this trend while reflecting cultural and societal values.*

3. **Assess Authenticity:** *Evaluate whether the messaging feels genuine and aligns with brand values.*

4. **Present a Tagline:** *Create a powerful, memorable tagline to reinforce your message.*

7.3 The Influence of Generational Values

Advertising works when you understand the unique values, preferences, and habits of your target audience. These are often shaped by the social, economic, and technological conditions of the generation they grew up in. By tailoring your campaigns to each generation's characteristics, you can create relevance, trust, and emotional connections that drive loyalty.

7.3.1. Generational Profiles in Advertising

1. **Baby Boomers (1946–1964):** This generation is devoted to companies that communicate with them and seek goods that provide reliability and long-term value. For this generation, successful advertising frequently emphasizes the longevity of the product, alludes to common cultural experiences, and emphasizes customer service and credibility.

For instance, the non-profit organization AARP, which serves Americans aged 50 and over, produces ads that discuss lifetime learning, trust, financial security, and health solutions. Review their ad in the Online Resources section, "What is AARP?"

2. **Generation X (1965–1980):** This generation values practicality, independence, and authenticity. Raised in an era that emphasized self-reliance, they like practical solutions and are turned off by sales-y advertising. Instead, they respond to humor and real messaging. To advertise to Gen X, brands should offer products that save time or simplify life, use relatable and straightforward communication, and appeal to their practicality with value-driven offers.

   Toyota designs ads that connect with this generation through safety, practicality, and affordability. Review their ad in the Online Resources section, "Chameleon Casting - Toyota Corolla: Never Stop Smiling."

3. **Millennials (1981–1996):** They value experiences over materialism and social consciousness and are fully immersed in the digital world. As digital natives, they look for convenience, personalization, and brands that reflect their values. They are more likely to share experiences than buy material goods and are drawn to companies that show social responsibility. Effective advertising for Millennials often involves storytelling that talks about a brand's purpose and community impact, personalized content delivered through digital tools like social media and apps, and promotions that focus on experiences.

Airbnb produces ads that highlight unique travel experiences and the power of human connection. Review their ad in the Online Resources section, "1/2 Billion Guest Arrival | Belong Anywhere."

4. **Gen Z (1997–2012):** Their core values are diversity, authenticity, and bold social activism. They value transparency, inclusivity, and brands that take a stand on social issues. Gen Z prefers interactive, visually driven content and often looks to peer approval when making decisions. To advertise to this generation, brands should show inclusive and diverse representation in their ads, use platforms like TikTok and Instagram for engagement, and align their messaging with social movements to show shared values.

Fenty Beauty, for example, demonstrates this well on their social platforms. Review their ad in the Online Resources section, "Fenty Beauty Campaign."

Exercise 7.2: Generational Persona Development

- *Build a detailed profile of a fictional customer from one of the four generations.*
- *Include their habits, values, and preferred communication styles.*
- *Design a product or service pitch specifically for that persona.*

Exercise 7.3: Cultural Adaptation Challenge

Take an ad campaign designed for one generation in a specific region and:

- *Adapt it for a different generation in another cultural context.*

- *Consider the values, preferences, and societal influences of both the target generation and their cultural background.*

In Conclusion

Culture and society are big forces that shape how brands talk to their audience. Good advertising requires cultural sensitivity, an understanding of societal trends, and the ability to adapt messaging to generational values. By getting these dynamics right, brands can connect with diverse audiences, build loyalty, and avoid mistakes in a globalized world.

Chapter Summary

- Advertising works when it fits with cultural norms, traditions, and symbols and creates an emotional connection. Misstep, and you get alienation or backlash.

- Societal values are evolving – inclusivity, sustainability, and activism are shaping advertising strategies, and brands need to stay relevant and socially aware.

- Each generation has its own preferences and values. Baby Boomers want reliability, and Gen Z wants diversity and social activism. Good campaigns reflect that.

- Global brands succeed by adapting to local customs, languages, and tastes and making sure the campaign resonates with the local audience (e.g., McDonald's and KFC).

- Campaigns must not be misinterpreted by looking at messaging through a global lens, as seen with Nivea's "White is Purity" campaign.

- Technology is becoming more and more prevalent in society, so we need to integrate digital innovation – interactive features and social media-driven campaigns.

- Knowing culture and society is key to creating ads that work, stay relevant, and avoid pitfalls in multiple markets.

Quiz

1. **What is the primary purpose of adapting advertising to cultural norms?**

   a. To reduce production costs
   b. To establish strong emotional connections
   c. To simplify brand messaging
   d. To minimize the need for localization

2. **Why did McDonald's introduce vegetarian options like the McAloo Tikki in India?**

   a. To attract international tourists
   b. To cater to health-conscious consumers
   c. To respect local religious and cultural preferences
   d. To compete with local street food vendors

3. **Which societal trend focuses on showcasing eco-friendly practices in advertising?**

   a. Inclusivity
   b. Activism
   c. Sustainability
   d. Digital integration

4. **What generational group prioritizes diversity, authenticity, and bold social activism?**

   a. Baby Boomers
   b. Generation X
   c. Millennials
   d. Gen Z

5. What lesson can advertisers learn from Nivea's "White is Purity" campaign controversy?
    a. Humor is universally understood in advertising.
    b. Cultural sensitivity should be evaluated through a global lens.
    c. Simplistic messaging avoids backlash.
    d. Apologies are unnecessary in advertising.

6. Which of the following best describes the influence of societal values on advertising?
    a. Societal values remain constant and don't affect trends.
    b. Ads ignore societal changes to maintain brand identity.
    c. Ads evolve alongside societal movements to remain relevant.
    d. Ads are completely unaffected by societal values.

7. What key factor contributed to KFC's success in China after its initial slogan translation error?
    a. Reducing product prices
    b. Localizing flavors and tastes
    c. Removing its slogan altogether
    d. Partnering with local fast-food brands

8. What is a significant characteristic of Millennial consumers in advertising?
    a. Preference for traditional advertising
    b. Desire for eco-friendly and socially conscious brands
    c. Focus on materialism over experiences
    d. Avoidance of digital platforms

9. Why is digital integration important in modern advertising?
   a. It reduces production costs.
   b. It simplifies campaign messaging.
   c. It aligns with society's reliance on technology.
   d. It eliminates the need for traditional media.

10. What does inclusivity in advertising involve?
    a. Including diverse casting and storytelling
    b. Using a single global message for all regions
    c. Focusing solely on the majority demographic
    d. Avoiding the use of local cultural symbols

Answers

1 – b	2 – c	3 – c	4 – d	5 – b
6 – c	7 – b	8 – b	9 – c	10 – a

Case Study 1: McDonald's - Adapting to Local Cultures (India)

Entering the Indian market was a big challenge for McDonald's as the country's cultural and religious landscape is so different from their traditional Western customer base. In a population where a large majority practice religions like Hinduism and Islam, beef and pork are sensitive or prohibited foods. To succeed in this space, McDonald's showed cultural intelligence and adaptability by rethinking their menu, operations, and marketing to suit local values.

How McDonald's Adapted to the Indian Market

Cultural and Religious Sensitivity

McDonald's knew that traditional Western staples like the Big Mac (made with beef) would not work with a large part of the Indian population. So they went for a culturally sensitive approach:

- The menu has only chicken, fish, and vegetarian options to cater to religious dietary restrictions.
- They introduced separate vegetarian and non-vegetarian preparation areas, utensils, and staff training to ensure dietary preferences are met.

Tailored Menu Offerings

McDonald's created new menu items inspired by Indian flavours and dietary habits:

- **McAloo Tikki Burger:** A potato patty with Indian spices for the vegetarian crowd.
- **Paneer Wraps:** Paneer (Indian cottage cheese) in wraps to offer a familiar protein source.

- **Masala Grill Chicken Burger:** A taste of the Indian love for spices and bold flavours.

- **Rice Bowls:** Rice-based meals to appeal beyond the traditional fast food offerings.

These local products helped the brand balance global and local.

Affordable Pricing

McDonald's recognized that affordability was crucial in India's price-sensitive market. They introduced smaller portion sizes and value combos to make their offerings accessible to a wider audience, especially among the burgeoning middle class.

Marketing and Messaging

McDonald's India tailored its marketing strategies to resonate with local consumers:

- Ads often emphasize family and togetherness, reflecting Indian cultural values.

- Campaigns highlight vegetarian options to appeal to the 30% of the population that identifies as vegetarian.

- Local festivals and holidays are leveraged in promotional efforts to build emotional connections with customers.

Localization of Operations

McDonald's partnered with local suppliers to source ingredients like paneer, spices, and vegetables. This not only reduced costs but also demonstrated a commitment to supporting the local economy.

Challenges Faced and Lessons Learned

- Created separate marketing strategies for the north, south, east, and west of India because of the country's diversity.
- They faced resistance from patrons wary of Western brands. They incorporated local culture into their brand to get around this.

Impact of Cultural Adaptation

McDonald's has more than 300 locations throughout India, demonstrating its enormous success there. In an area where international companies frequently fail, McDonald's prevailed by honoring cultural values and making adjustments to the market.

Key Takeaways

- **Cultural Sensitivity Drives Acceptance:** Understanding and respecting cultural and religious values is critical for brand success in diverse markets.
- **Localization Doesn't Compromise Global Identity:** McDonald's maintained its global brand while embracing local tastes and preferences.
- **Operational Adaptation is Key:** Changes in menu offerings, kitchen operations, and sourcing can make a brand more culturally relevant and trusted.
- **Affordable Pricing Matters:** Catering to the local economy ensures accessibility and brand loyalty.

Source: (BBC, 2014)

Case Study 2: KFC – "Finger-Lickin' Good" in China

In 1987, KFC entered China and faced many linguistic, cultural, and gastronomic challenges. Through quick

166 / Modern Advertising Essentials

adaptation, localization, and understanding of Chinese consumer behavior, KFC not only overcame the initial hurdles but became one of the most successful fast food chains in China.

Key Adaptations and Strategies

The "Finger-Lickin' Good" Slogan Mistranslation

During the initial campaign, this slogan was mistranslated into Mandarin, which literally means "Eat your fingers off." This mistranslation confused and turned off Chinese consumers, as it was funny but unintentionally gross.

KFC quickly changed the translation and shifted its focus to localized messaging. The new slogan was about the brand's quality and taste and was more in line with Chinese cultural norms. This early win showed KFC could adapt and listen to its audience.

Adapting the Menu to Local Tastes

Adapting the Menu to Local Tastes, KFC knew that winning in China was more than just language. Chinese consumers have different eating habits rooted in different regional cuisines. To cater to these tastes, KFC introduced:

- **Sichuan-Spiced Chicken:** To cater to the love for spicy food, especially in the Sichuan and Chongqing regions.
- **Congee (Rice Porridge):** A breakfast staple in China, KFC offers chicken congee to fit traditional eating habits.
- **Beijing Duck Wraps:** Inspired by the local iconic dish, this showed KFC can adapt famous recipes.
- **Herbal Soups:** KFC introduced soups inspired by traditional Chinese medicine to cater to health-conscious consumers.

This menu localization helped KFC to position themselves as a brand that respects and celebrates Chinese culinary heritage while staying true to themselves.

Strategic Market Positioning

KFC changed its positioning to family dining, which fits with the collectivist nature of Chinese society.

- Larger restaurants have more seating for families and groups.
- Advertisements showed shared meals and family gatherings to create emotional connections.

Operational Localization

To be more local, KFC localized its supply chain and operations:

- Sourcing locally reduced costs and built trust with consumers.
- Partnering with local suppliers showed KFC's commitment to China.

Marketing Campaigns That Resonate

KFC participated in Chinese cultural festivals and traditions:

- **Chinese New Year Promotions:** Limited-time menu items and festive packaging showed KFC's cultural relevance.
- **Digital Integration:** KFC used popular Chinese social media platforms, WeChat and Weibo, to reach younger audiences and promote offers.

Overcoming Challenges

Despite the end result, KFC faced intense competition from local brands and initial skepticism towards Western fast food. By localizing the menu, adapting the marketing, and addressing language mistakes early on, KFC became a trusted and familiar brand in China.

Impact of Localization

With more than 8,000 locations, KFC is currently the biggest and most prosperous fast-food brand in China. It has outperformed rivals like McDonald's in the area, mostly due to its capacity to modify its messaging and products to fit Chinese cultural standards.

Key Takeaways

- **Language Precision is Critical:** A mistranslation like "Finger Lickin' Good" can damage a brand. Get it right.
- **Menu Customization Drives Success:** Products inspired by local tastes are relevant and build loyalty.
- **Respect Local Culture:** Show cultural sensitivity to get accepted in new markets.
- **Strategic Marketing Matters:** Campaigns that fit with local traditions and festivals create emotional connections.

Source: Beach, 2022

Case Study 3: Nivea – "White is Purity" Campaign Controversy (Germany)

With their "White is Purity" ad in 2017, the multinational skincare company Nivea fell into trouble. The ad was meant to promote a deodorant, and through this, it was supposed to promote cleanliness and simplicity. But it was seen as racist, especially in a globalized social media world. This is a classic example of cultural blindness in advertising and why brands need to look through a global and inclusive lens.

The Campaign and Its Context

Campaign Objective

Nivea wanted to use "White is Purity" to represent the characteristics of their products:

- **Cleanliness:** The phrase was meant to be the purity and freshness of white clothes after using the deodorant.

- **Simplicity:** Nivea's minimalist and clean branding, which means reliability and trust.

The campaign was launched in Europe and the Middle East, where white is culturally associated with cleanliness, neutrality, and purity.

The Controversy

The phrase "White is Purity" went viral, and Nivea was accused of being racist. In a world where racial equity and diversity are hot topics, the phrase was seen as promoting racial supremacy, especially in markets outside of the intended geography.

- The phrase became a trending topic on platforms like Twitter, with users drawing connections to white supremacist ideologies.

- While the campaign may have aligned with European perceptions of white as a symbol of cleanliness, in other markets, the messaging was perceived as tone-deaf and offensive.

How Nivea Responded

Immediate Action

- Nivea pulled the ad and apologized publicly, admitting the mistake.

- The brand said the slogan was meant to be about simplicity and purity, not race.

Lessons Learned

Nivea's quick response limited the damage, but this was a wake-up call for the company to get more sophisticated with global advertising.

Key Lessons from the Controversy

- **Messaging Must Be Evaluated in a Global Context:** A slogan that works in one market can mean something entirely different in another. "White is Purity" might be a play on the German idea of white as cleanliness, but in multicultural and race-sensitive markets, it can have unintended and harmful connotations.

- **Diverse Perspectives in Campaign Development:** This shows the importance of diverse teams and inclusive thinking in campaign development. Having people who understand different cultural sensitivities involved could have prevented the backlash.

- **The Power of Social Media:** In today's world, advertising is not limited to one market. A misstep in one region can go global, and the backlash will be amplified. Brands need to be prepared for this.

- **Apologies Matter, but Prevention is Better:** While Nivea's quick apology mitigated some of the damage, the controversy affected the brand's reputation. Proactive cultural sensitivity checks are more effective than damage control after the fact.

Impact on Nivea's Branding

The controversy prompted Nivea to reevaluate its approach to advertising and branding, particularly in international markets:

- Nivea implemented stricter review processes for global campaigns to avoid future missteps.

- The company publicly committed to promoting inclusivity in its branding and operations.

While the backlash was a significant moment for the brand, it also provided an opportunity for growth and introspection, forcing Nivea to align with evolving consumer expectations around diversity and sensitivity.

Key Takeaway

What resonates in one culture can offend in another. Brands operating in diverse markets must evaluate their campaigns through a global lens, ensuring their messaging is free from unintended biases or insensitivity. This includes engaging diverse teams, conducting thorough cultural audits, and testing campaigns across different regions before launch.

Source: (Tsang, 2017)

Exercise: Designing a Culturally Adapted Campaign

- *Imagine a fast-food chain entering a new cultural market. Design a localized menu, operational change, and a marketing campaign that respects the cultural and religious values of the target audience.*

- *Present your strategy to a group, including key adaptations, expected challenges, and how your campaign will address them.*

By taking inspiration from McDonald's example in India, this exercise will help you understand the complexities of entering culturally diverse markets.

Further Learning

Links also available in Online Resources:

1. **Kendall Jenner Pepsi Ad**
   http://bit.ly/3GW67nA

2. **H&M's "Coolest Monkey in the Jungle" Incident**
   http://bit.ly/4IJSmri

3. **What is AARP?**
   http://bit.ly/4mdFYQd

4. **Chameleon Casting - Toyota Corolla 'Never Stop Smiling'**
   http://bit.ly/4ma7Uo6

5. **1/2 Billion Guest Arrival | Belong Anywhere**
   http://bit.ly/3TQvR7N

6. **Fenty Beauty Campaign**
   http://bit.ly/3GNoMSx

CHAPTER 8

Navigating Ethics in Advertising

Key Learning Objectives

- How to recognize the consequences of misleading customers and the significance of telling the truth in advertising.
- How to analyze targeted advertising and data privacy ethical concerns while adhering to international laws.
- The difference between manipulation and ethical persuasion, as well as when marketing strategies go beyond moral bounds.
- Real-world advertising campaigns, both ethical and unethical.
- How to create responsible advertising that builds trust, loyalty, and long-term success.

Perceptions, choices, and behavior can all be influenced by advertising. But how is deception different from marketing? Brands have to negotiate the tricky ethical terrain of advertising at a time when credibility is vital.

This chapter looks at the ethical dilemmas in advertising, such as how to balance consumer privacy, messaging truth, and persuasion and manipulation. You will learn how to assess and produce ethical and successful advertising through practical exercises, ethical successes and failures, and real-world case studies.

8.1 Keeping It Real: Why Truth Matters in Advertising

Consumers expect the companies they buy from to be honest with them. False claims make short-term gains, but long-term trust is lost.

The risks far outweigh the benefits, despite the temptation to exaggerate or mislead. In the short term, misleading ads may make more money, but there are huge consequences, lawsuits, a decline in consumer trust, and irreversible damage to the brand. If you get caught misleading your customers, you could face fines, loss of market share, and a reputation that's hard to repair.

8.1.2 Advertising Regulations and Ethical Standards

In numerous countries, honesty in advertising is mandated by law, leaving no alternative but to act ethically. Ethical advertising reduces the likelihood of legal and financial consequences while promoting trust and compliance.

Numerous regulatory organizations exist to safeguard consumers against deceptive advertising and unsupported assertions. Some notable agencies are:

1. **The Federal Trade Commission (FTC):** The FTC in the U.S. enforces regulations concerning deceptive or false

advertising. In the U.K., the Advertising Standards Authority (ASA) maintains principles of integrity, equity, and social responsibility.

2. **General Data Protection Regulation (GDPR):** Right next door, the GDPR in the European Union influences digital advertising by requiring companies to secure users' explicit consent before collecting and using their personal data for advertising purposes.

3. **California Consumer Privacy Act (CCPA):** The CCPA grants consumers rights akin to those in the GDPR, including the option to opt out of data sales for advertising purposes and to receive information about the personal data gathered.

8.1.3 When Advertising Crosses the Line

1. **Volkswagen – "Dieselgate"**

   Here's a famous instance of false advertising: Volkswagen's "Dieselgate." They promoted their diesel vehicles as environmentally friendly, featuring low emissions and excellent fuel economy.

   However, it was subsequently discovered that they had implemented software to manipulate the emissions tests, causing their vehicles to appear far more environmentally friendly than they actually were.

   The consequences were significant fines, legal actions, and a considerable decline in consumer confidence. Watch the overview for more in Online Resources under Volkswagen Dieselgate.

2. **Kim Kardashian - Flat Tummy Tea**

   An additional instance is Kim Kardashian endorsing Flat Tummy Tea. Kardashian, a well-known influencer, promoted detox teas that asserted to aid in weight loss and digestion. However, the endorsements misrepresented the health advantages, failing to reveal the dangers: dehydration, digestive issues, and lack of scientific support.

The campaign faced criticism for endorsing unrealistic body standards and misleading consumers, particularly the younger demographic. Watch the overview for more in the Online Resources under Kim Kardashian.

These instances demonstrate that ethical advertising matters. While an instant gain might be appealing, the future effects can negatively impact both the brand and the consumer. Figure 8.1 below provides a summary of common consequences of unethical practices in advertising.

Figure 8.1 **Common Consequences of Unethical Practices in Advertising**

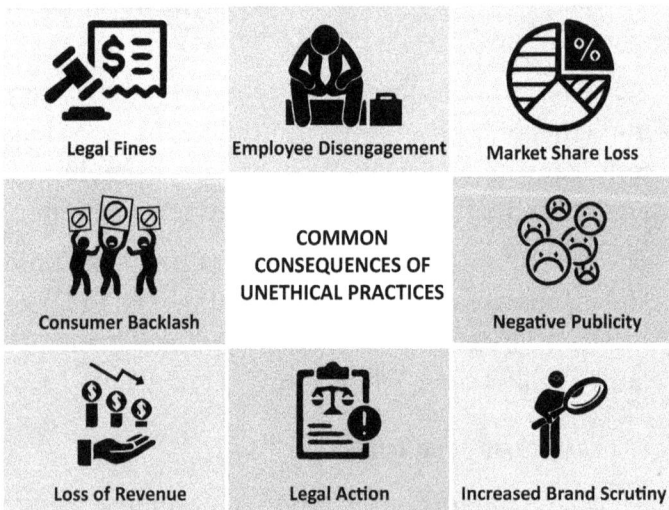

Legal Fines

Employee Disengagement

Market Share Loss

Consumer Backlash

COMMON CONSEQUENCES OF UNETHICAL PRACTICES

Negative Publicity

Loss of Revenue

Legal Action

Increased Brand Scrutiny

8.1.4 Ethical Advertising in Action

Successful brands recognize that transparency fosters loyalty, which is built on more than just good products, as today's consumers want honesty and will reward you for it. Information can be found a mere click away, making it easy for customers to spot what's real and what's not. Brands that are open about their practices, values, and even faults can establish higher levels of engagement with their market. Consider the example of TOMS's "One for One" initiative.

Having launched in 2006, the concept was straightforward but impactful. For each pair of shoes bought, TOMS would provide one pair to a child in need. What distinguished TOMS was not merely the charitable deed but the profound transparency integrated into its business model. The company transparently shared how customer purchases resulted in social impact, creating a strong sense of trust and genuineness.

TOMS regularly communicated stories, visuals, and updates from its donation initiatives, enabling customers to witness the real impact of their buying decisions. This openness not only made the brand more relatable but also turned customers into engaged participants in a worldwide mission, fostering emotional ties that went beyond conventional buyer- seller dynamics.

Nonetheless, the brand's path also emphasizes the challenges of ethical marketing. In subsequent years, TOMS encountered scrutiny over the lasting sustainability of its donation approach, with certain experts claiming that shoe donations might inadvertently harm local economies. Rather than disregarding these issues, TOMS adapted its strategy, moving towards impact grants and initiatives driven by the community.

This readiness to recognize deficiencies and adjust strengthened its dedication to ethical standards.

TOMS's journey highlights an important lesson: transparency isn't merely a marketing tactic; it's a continuous obligation that demands brands remain accountable, even during difficult times. (Mycoskie, 2011)

Exercise 8.1: Ethical Ad Analysis

Find three advertisements (TV, print, or digital). Analyze their ethical implications by asking the following:

- *Are they truthful?*
- *Do they respect cultural and societal values?*
- *Do they responsibly handle consumer data or emotions?*

Write a short analysis explaining why each ad is ethical or unethical.

8.2 Your Data, Your Rights: Privacy in the Ad World

The digital era has transformed advertising, positioning personal data as the core of targeted marketing efforts. Nonetheless, the ethical utilization of consumer data is an increasing issue. Brands need to find a balance between personalization and respect for privacy, ensuring adherence to regulations such as the General Data Protection Regulation (GDPR) and the California Consumer Privacy Act (CCPA).

8.2.1. Ethical Data Practices

Companies that emphasize user privacy adhere to the guidelines outlined in Figure 8.2 below. They are as follows:

- **Clear Consent:** Users are required to explicitly consent to data gathering.

- **Clarity:** Explicitly describe the methods of data collection, storage, and utilization.

- **Choices to Opt-Out:** Users ought to have authority over data monitoring.

- **Data Security:** Safeguarding personal information is essential.

Figure 8.2 The Four Pillars of Ethical Data Practices in Advertising

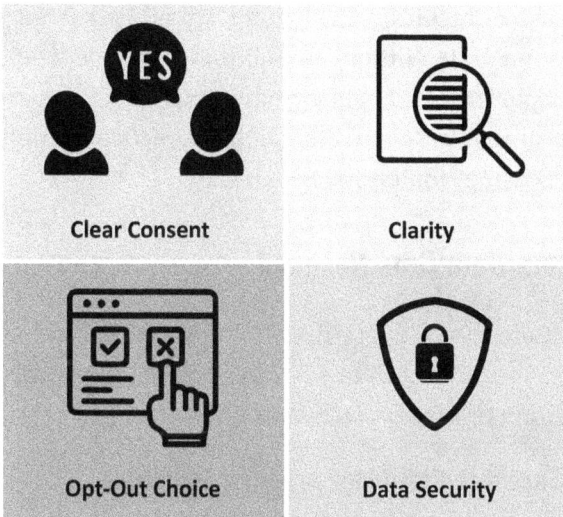

Clear Consent

Clarity

Opt-Out Choice

Data Security

8.2.2. Brands Pioneering Data Ethics

Certain companies have integrated privacy into their essential brand commitment, understanding that consumer confidence relies on data security and openness.

1. **Apple:** Via initiatives such as "Privacy. That's iPhone.", Apple assures users that their personal data stays protected, establishing a standard for ethical data practices in the industry. By introducing elements such as App Tracking Transparency and on-device processing, Apple shows that privacy can serve as a competitive benefit. (Grothaus, 2019)

2. **Mozilla Firefox:** Firefox has consistently championed internet privacy, incorporating functionalities that enable users to manage their online information by hindering intrusive tracking, which stops advertisers from gathering personal data without permission. Their dedication to transparency and user empowerment sets it apart as a leading example of ethical data practices in online advertising. (Battaglia, 2024)

8.2.3. When Data Gets Misused

Nevertheless, not every brand maintains ethical principles. Prominent data scandals underscore the repercussions of inadequate data practices:

- **Facebook-Cambridge Analytica Scandal**
  This situation revealed the improper use of millions of Facebook accounts for political ads, highlighting issues related to data transparency. (Kozlowska, 2018)

- **Google Street View Data Leak**
  Google gathered personal Wi-Fi information without obtaining user permission, leading to regulatory fines. (BBC News, 2013)

Exercise 8.2: Rewriting the Scandal

Research an ad campaign that faced backlash for unethical practices. Rewrite the campaign to align with ethical advertising principles.

- *What changes would you make?*
- *How does your version improve transparency and consumer trust?*

8.3 The Fine Line: Persuasion vs. Manipulation in Advertising

Persuasive advertising sways consumers to take action, yet ethical marketing steers clear of manipulation. Persuasion relies on truthfulness and worth, whereas manipulation takes advantage of psychological weaknesses to boost sales.

8.3.1. Understanding the Difference

Advertising can influence consumer behavior significantly, yet it is important to differentiate between ethical persuasion and manipulation. Persuasion is a vital marketing resource that educates, encourages, and drives consumers to choose wisely. It offers precise information and matches consumer preferences and principles. Manipulation, conversely, takes advantage of emotions, twists reality, and coerces consumers into making decisions they may not normally contemplate.

Table 8.1 below illustrates the key differences between persuasion and manipulation.

Table 8.1	Persuasion versus Manipulation in Marketing
Persuasion	Manipulation
Informs and inspires	Creates artificial urgency
Uses truthful messaging	Exploits emotions (fear, guilt)
Encourages informed decisions	Withholds or distorts information

8.3.2. Persuasion: Ethical Influence in Advertising

Persuasive advertising enables consumers to recognize the worth of a product or service without deceiving them. It emphasizes honest communication, emotional engagement, and empowerment, enabling customers to make informed decisions.

Brands have the ability to motivate and encourage consumer engagement without the need for trickery. Ethical advertising emphasizes constructive messaging, empowering consumers instead of deceiving them.

1. **Always: "#LikeAGirl" Initiative** – The initiative transformed a familiar expression to confront gender stereotypes and empower young women. The campaign promoted self-belief and broke down outdated societal norms by depicting girls confidently and powerfully engaging in various tasks. This method struck a chord with audiences, demonstrating that uplifting messages can generate social influence and foster brand loyalty. (Always, n.d)

2. **The Body Shop: Responsible Consumer Behavior** – Established its credibility through ethical business methods, persistently supporting cruelty-free and eco-friendly

products. By communicating clearly about sustainability and animal welfare, the brand connects with consumer values, showing that ethical persuasion can serve as an effective instrument for marketing and fostering positive change. (The Body Shop, n.d)

8.3.3. Manipulation: When Advertising Goes Too Far

In contrast, manipulative advertising aims to influence consumer behavior using fear, guilt, or false information. It frequently generates fake urgency, misrepresents facts, or hides important information to compel consumers into quick decision-making.

Ethical advertising builds trust and engagement, whereas unethical practices can greatly harm a brand's reputation. Manipulative advertisements frequently take advantage of feelings, misrepresent the truth, or employ misleading assertions to boost sales. Some instances include:

1. **Fyre Festival Influencer Ads:** Promoted as an extremely lavish festival in the Bahamas, Fyre Festival leveraged influencer marketing to attract participants by touting exclusive experiences and celebrity performances. In truth, the occasion was chaotically disorganized, leaving ticket purchasers abandoned with insufficient arrangements. This obvious fraud not only caused significant financial losses but also resulted in legal repercussions for the organizers. (Cohn, 2019)

2. **Cigarette Ads (20th Century):** For many years, cigarette companies misleadingly advertised smoking as chic, refined, and even helpful for health. Ads showcased doctors promoting cigarettes, bolstering the false sense of safety while minimizing serious health dangers. The consequences of this unethical marketing strategy led to

widespread addiction and lasting health issues prior to the implementation of regulations.

Today, consumers are more knowledgeable than they have ever been. As awareness of manipulative marketing rises, brands that partake in deceitful practices encounter public criticism and backlash. Conversely, businesses that emphasize integrity and ethical influence foster enduring loyalty, demonstrating that honesty is not merely a moral duty but also a tactical benefit.

Exercise 8.3: Privacy Policy Review

Visit the privacy policies of three major companies (e.g., Apple, Facebook, Amazon). Compare their data collection and transparency practices.

- *Which policy is most ethical?*
- *How does it prioritize consumer rights?*

Write a brief comparison outlining your findings.

In Conclusion

Ethical advertising is not only a moral duty but a strategic requirement in today's consumer-oriented market. Clarity, consideration for privacy, and ethical persuasion are the foundations of advertising that foster trust and enduring brand loyalty. Firms that emphasize integrity and customer welfare enhance their reputation, whereas those that partake in misleading tactics face the danger of backlash, legal consequences, and diminished credibility.

As digital marketing advances, ethical concerns will stay central, influencing how brands interact with their audiences. By adopting ethical advertising principles, companies can build significant relationships, encourage wise choices, and aid in creating a more accountable marketing environment.

Chapter Summary

- Ethical advertising fosters consumer trust and safeguards brand reputation, whereas misleading ads may result in legal repercussions and public outrage.

- Businesses should be transparent regarding product features, costs, and possible constraints to prevent deceiving customers.

- Regulations like the FTC's Truth in Advertising rules and the ASA's UK advertising guidelines promote fairness and deter deceptive advertising practices.

- Online advertising depends on personal information, which makes privacy laws (GDPR, CCPA) crucial for safeguarding consumer rights. Ethical brands guarantee clarity, approval, and safety in data utilization.

- Ethical persuasion motivates consumers through honest communication, whereas manipulation takes advantage of feelings such as fear and guilt.

- Today's consumers are well-informed and appreciate genuine authenticity. Responsible advertising not only avoids legal issues but also promotes enduring brand loyalty and trust.

- Companies such as LEGO (emphasizing sustainability) exhibit ethical leadership, whereas missteps like Dove's 2017 Body Wash advertisement showcase the dangers of badly crafted communication.

Quiz

1. **Why is truth important in advertising?**
   a. It increases immediate sales.
   b. It builds long-term consumer trust and credibility.
   c. It allows brands to avoid competition.
   d. It ensures higher profit margins.

2. **Which of the following is an example of truthful advertising?**
   a. Patagonia's Campaign
   b. Volkswagen's Dieselgate
   c. Kim Kardashian's Flat Tummy Tea ad
   d. Fyre Festival promotions

3. **What was the main issue with Volkswagen's Dieselgate?**
   a. Overpricing their vehicles
   b. Falsely marketing their vehicles as eco-friendly
   c. Failing to launch new models on time
   d. Not offering financing options

4. **Which regulation aims to prevent deceptive advertising?**
   a. GDPR
   b. CCPA
   c. FTC Truth in Advertising laws
   d. DMCA

5. What was the ethical issue with Kim Kardashian's Flat Tummy Tea ad?

   a. It contained banned substances.
   b. It was only available in limited countries.
   c. The tea was too expensive.
   d. It lacked proper disclaimers about health risks.

6. Which regulation gives users more control over their personal data in the European Union?

   a. DMCA
   b. CCPA
   c. FTC Act
   d. GDPR

7. Which company has positioned itself as a leader in user privacy with the slogan "Privacy. That's iPhone."?

   a. Apple
   b. Google
   c. Facebook
   d. Amazon

8. What was the major ethical concern in the Facebook-Cambridge Analytica scandal?

   a. Blocking competitor advertisements
   b. False advertising of Facebook products
   c. Unauthorized sharing of user data for political purposes
   d. Selling user accounts on the dark web

9. Which company is known for its strong stance on user privacy and tracking protection?
   a. Mozilla Firefox
   b. Microsoft Edge
   c. TikTok
   d. Uber

10. How can brands ensure ethical data collection?
    a. By obtaining explicit user consent
    b. By using vague privacy policies
    c. By sharing user data with third parties freely
    d. By tracking users without informing them

Answers

1 – b	2 – a	3 – b	4 – c	5 – d
6 – d	7 – a	8 – c	9 – a	10 – a

Case Study 1: Ethical Win - LEGO (Sustainability Focus)

LEGO's commitment to sustainability goes beyond environmental concerns. It is ingrained in the brand's fundamental values, promoting consumer trust and loyalty.

Acknowledging the ecological consequences of plastic production, LEGO began to alter its methods towards responsible and sustainable practices, establishing a standard for the toy sector.

In 2015, LEGO declared its aim to eliminate petroleum-derived plastics from its products by 2030. This initiated a major investment in research for sustainable materials, with over $400 million designated for environmental projects.

Notable progress was made with the introduction of LEGO bricks made from polyethylene sourced from sugarcane, a robust and eco-friendly plastic.

Although these new materials were first used for softer products like trees, leaves, and accessories, LEGO is working to guarantee they fulfill the durability standards for its traditional bricks.

Alongside sustainable materials, LEGO has achieved notable progress in renewable energy. In 2017, LEGO reached its objective of operating entirely on renewable energy, a notable achievement realized through considerable investments in wind power, notably through co-ownership of the Burbo Bank Extension offshore wind farm located in the UK.

Source: (LEGO Group, 2018)

Case Study 2: Ethical Fail: Dove's Body Wash Ad (2017)

Dove, a brand well-known for promoting body positivity and inclusivity with campaigns such as "Real Beauty", became embroiled in a significant controversy in 2017 following the launch of a body wash advertisement on Facebook.

The advertisement showcased a brief video in which a Black woman took off her brown top to uncover a White woman beneath, succeeded by an Asian woman. Aimed at honoring diversity by highlighting various women, the realization of the idea failed dramatically.

Numerous viewers perceived the visuals as reinforcing a damaging racial narrative—implying that Black skin required "cleansing" to unveil a superior, lighter skin tone beneath.

The response was immediate and fierce. Social media erupted with criticism, accusing Dove of racial insensitivity and a lack of awareness. The brand, once recognized as a champion for diversity and self-acceptance, confronted claims of promoting the stereotypes it claimed to stand against.

The event ignited extensive conversations regarding the ingrained challenges of race in advertising and the impact of visual storytelling on influencing cultural views.

Dove promptly reacted by pulling the advertisement and delivering a public apology. The company asserted that the campaign aimed to honor diversity and highlight the beauty of various skin types without suggesting any type of racial hierarchy.

Nonetheless, the harm to the brand's image had already occurred. This event was especially harmful since it wasn't

Dove's first encounter with criticism regarding racially inappropriate advertisements.

Dove's controversy emphasizes an important difference between a brand's intention and the perception of its message. Although an advertisement may be designed with good intentions, neglecting cultural sensitivities can lead to negative effects on varied audiences. In advertising, how something is perceived frequently surpasses the intended message.

The Significance of Varied Perspectives

Insufficient diversity in creative teams may cause blind spots that produce offensive material. If a wider range of viewpoints had been incorporated during the concept development and review stages, it's probable that the issues with the ad would have been recognized prior to its release. Inclusive marketing goes beyond representation in advertisements; it involves including diverse decision-makers in the process.

The Importance of Crisis Management

Although Dove's prompt apology alleviated some of the repercussions, the repeated occurrence of these problems indicated a trend rather than a singular event. In crisis management, tackling the underlying issue, like deficiencies in internal diversity or insufficient training in cultural competency, is as crucial as making public declarations.

The Influence of Social Media

In the digital era, advertisements can become viral for negative reasons within a few hours. Social media magnifies both commendation and critique, making it crucial for brands to engage in cultural consciousness. Dove's situation illustrates how fast public opinion can change from praise to anger when a brand makes a mistake.

Key Takeaway

To prevent comparable mistakes, businesses should adopt inclusive marketing strategies, guarantee that campaigns are evaluated with cultural sensitivity, and cultivate atmospheres where varied perspectives are acknowledged and appreciated.

Source: (Astor, 2017)

Exercise: Ethics Audit: Analyzing Advertising Practices

Select a company and analyze its advertising strategies based on ethical principles. Consider the following:

1. **Transparency**
2. **Consumer Privacy**
3. **Persuasion vs. Manipulation**
4. **Social Responsibility**

Write a **500-word audit** detailing whether the company's advertising aligns with ethical standards or if improvements are needed.

Further Learning

Links also available in Online Resources

- **Volkswagen Dieselgate**
  http://bit.ly/4mcBBoA

- **Kim Kardashian**
  http://bit.ly/4lKAc8R

- **CBS News reporting on the Dove Campaign**
  http://bit.ly/4m1p32Y

CHAPTER 9

Numbers Don't Lie: Measuring Ad Success

Key Learning Objectives

- Key measures that marketers employ to monitor their advertisements
- Tools to measure the success of an advert
- How to interpret data to make smart decisions
- How A/B testing can lead to big improvements
- How well-known brands master data-driven advertising

Marketing is both an art form and a scientific discipline. Though creativity draws focus, data establishes success. In the digital era, advertisers must not depend solely on intuition. Achieving success relies on quantifiable results. Key performance metrics (KPIs) offer valuable information regarding audience interaction, advertising effectiveness, and return on investment (ROI), assisting marketers in refining their strategies promptly.

This chapter expands on the insights gained in Chapter 3 regarding advertising data, delving further into critical advertising metrics, tools for monitoring campaign success, and techniques for analyzing data to enhance ad performance. It also explores A/B testing, a robust method for optimizing ads for optimal effectiveness. By the conclusion of this chapter, you will be equipped to evaluate the effectiveness of advertising with assurance, utilizing data-informed decision-making.

9.1 Key Metrics 101

Knowing what to measure is the first step in gauging the success of your campaign. Below is some basic advertisement math that you need to know.

1. **Impressions**

   Impressions are the number of times an advertisement shows on a screen when an individual may scroll past an ad without clicking it.

   This metric is quite useful for brand awareness campaigns, which aim to expose as many people as possible to a brand rather than to push for clicks or sales. Say, for example, that a digital billboard from a sportswear brand runs 100,000 times; thereby, it has 100,000 impressions.

2. **Click-Through Rate (CTR)**

   CTR highlights the percentage of users who have seen an advert and clicked on it.

   The ad may need to be improved in some way if it has a low CTR score. These improvements may require changes to the headline, imagery, or user persona. If the CTR value for an ad is high, the marketing team may consider themselves successful and hold off on making changes to the campaign. See Figure 9.1 below for the Click-Through Rate Formula.

Figure 9.1 | Click-Through Rate Formula

$$Click\ Through\ Rate\ (CTR)(\%) = \left(\frac{Total\ Clicks}{Total\ Impressions}\right) \times 100$$

3. **Conversion Rate**

   Conversion could be anything like buying a product, subscribing to a newsletter, downloading an app, or simply just filling out a form.

   Conversion rate is the primary figure that gives insight into whether an ad is convincing users to do a particular task after it was clicked or not.

   A conversion rate is high when the ad attracts the right people and encourages them to take action. Low conversion rates might lead to issues on the landing page, product offering, or message of the ad. See Figure 9.2 below for the Conversion Rate Formula.

Figure 9.2 | Conversion Rate Formula

$$Conversion\ Rate\ (\%) = \left(\frac{Total\ Conversions}{Total\ Clicks}\right) \times 100$$

   If, let's say, 1,000 users clicked on an ad and 50% of them made a purchase, the conversion rate would be 5% since 5% of individuals who visited the ad ended up completing a purchase.

4. **Return on Investment (ROI)**

   ROI measures the return or profitability of an ad campaign by comparing revenues generated to a campaign's cost.

A positive ROI is a good thing! It means that the campaign brought in more money for the company than it spent paying the agency to produce the ad. A negative ROI signals doom because the finance team won't be impressed by what they may deem as wasteful expenditure. See Figure 9.3 below for the ROI Formula.

Figure 9.3   ROI Formula

$$Return\ on\ Investment\ (ROI)\ (\%) = \left(\frac{Revenue\ from\ Ads - Cost\ of\ Ads}{Cost\ of\ Ads}\right) \times 100$$

If an ad campaign costs $500 and generates $1,500 in revenue, the ROI is:

((1,500 - 500) / 500) x 100 = 200%

A 200% ROI means the campaign generated twice its initial investment in profit and may be worth highlighting come performance evaluation time.

5. **Cost Per Click (CPC)**

    CPC is where budgeting typically begins. It represents how much the company effectively spends for every click on its ad. The lower the CPC, the more clicks you get with less money, which is exactly what you need. You can also use CPC to compare costs across different platforms. See Figure 9.4 below for the Cost Per Click Formula.

Figure 9.4   Cost Per Click Formula

$$Cost\ Per\ Click = \left(\frac{Total\ Ad\ Spend}{Total\ Clicks}\right)$$

If an advertiser spends $200 on a campaign that generates 100 clicks, the CPC is (200 ÷ 100) = $2.00 per click.

6. **Cost Per Acquisition (CPA)**

The CPA tells how expensive it is to gain a new customer, meaning the amount a business has to spend to acquire one person who completes an action intended, such as purchasing or creating an account. CPA allows an advertiser to measure their campaign's efficiency.

A lower CPA will indicate that your targeting, messaging, and overall strategy are in tune and that you turned browsers into customers at relatively low costs. A high CPA can also mean your competition is strong, which hikes up advertising costs. See Figure 9.5 below for the Cost Per Acquisition Formula.

Figure 9.5 **Cost Per Acquisition Formula**

$$Cost\ Per\ Acquisition\ (CPA) = \left(\frac{Total\ Ad\ Spend}{Total\ Conversions} \right)$$

That would mean that an $800 campaign leads to 40 purchases, a CPA of $20 per acquisition — which ultimately means that each customer costs a business $20 to acquire.

7. **Cost Per Mille (CPM)**

CPM calculates the price for 1,000 ad views. In this case, branding is more important than clicks or sales.

Thus, brands that want to get the most audience — for example, when running a branded awareness campaign — invest more in CPM but save on CPC and CPA.

Naturally, the smaller the CPM, the more value a marketer gets because it reaches the most amount of people for fewer dollars. See Figure 9.6 below for the Cost Per Mille Formula.

Figure 9.6 Cost Per Mille Formula

$$\text{Cost Per Mille (CPM)} = \left(\frac{Total\,Ad\,Spend}{Total\,Impressions} \right) \times 1000$$

If an advertiser gets 100,000 impressions after spending $500 on an ad, the CPM is (500 ÷ 100,000) x 1000 = 5.

It literally means that it costs $5 to reach 1,000 people.

Exercise 9.1: Analyzing Metrics

We Bake u Happy is running advertising campaigns on Instagram and Facebook in an effort to attract more customers to the bakery. It wants to determine which channel provides a better return based on certain key metrics.

Here's the data for each of the campaigns:

Metric	Instagram Ad	Facebook Ad
Total Impressions	50,000	70,000
Total Clicks	1,000	1,200
Total Conversions	50	60
Total Ad Spend ($)	500	600

Assuming management is most concerned with the cost of acquiring new customers, calculate the CPA for the Instagram ad and the CPA for the Facebook ad, then explain which platform is yielding better results.

9.2 Tracking Tools: How to Use Google Analytics and Social Insights

Now that you can identify what to measure, how would you track these numbers? Thankfully, solid tools like Google Analytics and social media insights make it pretty easy to track your ad performance by providing real-time data on how to optimize your campaign with efficiency.

9.2.1 Google Analytics: Understanding Website Traffic

Google Analytics is powerful for tracking consumer behavior on a website once the ad has been clicked. Figure 9.7 below shows some of what this tool makes possible, such as the geographic location of where your visitors are coming from, what they are clicking on, and how they're interacting with your content.

Figure 9.7 Sample insights available from Google Analytics

	Traffic Analysis	Tracks where visitors come from (e.g. social media, search engines)
	Bounce Rate	Measures how many visitors leave a site without interacting further.
	Conversion Tracking	Records actions users take, such as purchases or sign-ups.

9.2.2 Social Media Insights: Engagement & Audience Behavior

Platforms like Facebook, Instagram, Twitter, and LinkedIn have in-built analytics that support you in identifying and measuring key data points like how many people viewed your ad (reach), who your audience is (age, gender, location), and how many engaged with it (likes, shares, comments).

By checking these insights regularly, you can refine your content and ensure that your messaging is framed correctly for your ideal audience.

Exercise 9.2: Using a Tracking Tool

1. *Access Google Analytics (or a social media analytics tool).*

2. *Identify an ad campaign and review its CTR, audience insights, and conversion rate.*

3. *Write a short analysis of its performance.*

9.3 Reading the Data to Improve Your Ads

Here's how you can get the most out of your data and use the insights it makes possible to inform your decision-making:

1. **Identify trends:** Regularly review ad performance over time to spot patterns. For example, are there certain days of the week that deliver better results? Do certain formats, such as videos, get more clicks?

2. **Match your messaging with your audience:** Different groups respond to the same content in different ways, and one must make sure to make the messaging more personal to each group. This means studying statistics to learn what works for each segment of your audience, adjusting tone and texture to fit their tastes, and paying attention to more personalization and less generic messaging.

3. **Make changes where the performance is not up to scratch:** A campaign with a combination of a high CTR and a low

conversion rate will require some action to ensure the best results.

4. **Review the results from the A/B Testing:** Comparing two versions of an ad reveals what works best. We will delve deeper into the process of A/B testing in the next section.

For example, the data from the latest smartwatch ad by a tech company shows that 18-24-year-olds have the highest conversion rate, while 25-34-year-olds have the highest engagement. That means older users like the ad, but younger users are buying the product. With this insight, they might shift their budget to target the younger audience more aggressively.

Exercise 9.3: Interpreting Ad Data

1. *Find an ad campaign report (or use a mock dataset).*

2. *Identify patterns in CTR, conversion rates, and audience engagement.*

3. *Suggest two improvements based on your findings.*

9.4 A/B Testing: Minor Adjustments, Major Outcomes

At times, small modifications can lead to significant effects. A/B testing is a method based on data for enhancing advertisements by experimenting with minor changes, like a headline, call-to-action, or image.

A/B testing, or split-testing, is a method based on data for enhancing advertisements by experimenting with minor changes, such as headlines, call-to-action buttons, images, or ad formats to optimize messages and designs based on real user wants rather than assumptions.

It is most effective when outcomes are contrasted directly. The key is to alter just a single variable at a time and leave all other variables consistent. That way, advertisers can say exactly which component impacted performance.

Let's say two ads use diverse images but the same text; we can reasonably assume that any variation in click-through rate (CTR) is attributable to the images. However, if multiple elements (such as the image, text, and CTA) are changed at once, it is hard to be sure which aspect had the greatest effect on the change in performance.

Example: A clothing retailer evaluates two Facebook advertisements:

- **Ad A:** "Spring Discount – 30% Off Every Product!"
- **Ad B:** "Discover the Finest of the Season – 30% Discount Today!"

After a week of running both ads, Ad A achieves a 4% CTR, whereas Ad B attains a 6% CTR.

Based on these stats, the retailer can confidently conclude that the messaging in Ad B is the most suitable for its audience. As a result, the retailer would do well to allocate more budget to the better-performing ad.

Exercise 9.4: Designing an A/B Test

1. *Choose an ad and identify one element to test (headline, image, CTA).*
2. *Write two variations.*
3. *Predict which will perform better and why.*

In Conclusion

Advertising has evolved from being merely creative and intuitive to a science rooted in data. The most successful brands consistently enhance their strategy and employ a mix of appealing visuals and memorable slogans, live data, audience insights, and A/B testing. By comprehending essential metrics, utilizing tracking tools, and experimenting with various strategies, advertisers can enhance engagement, boost conversions, and achieve optimal returns on their investments.

Chapter Summary

- Advertisers depend on impressions, CTR, conversion rates, ROI, CPC, CPA, and CPM to assess and enhance campaign performance.

- Google Analytics, along with social media insights, delivers immediate information on audience behavior, sources of traffic, and ad interaction, assisting advertisers in making educated choices.

- Metrics by themselves are insufficient; advertisers need to examine trends, pinpoint weaknesses, and modify their strategies to enhance campaign performance.

- By testing various ad formats, advertisers can enhance aspects such as headlines, imagery, and calls to action to boost engagement and conversion rates.

- A reduced Cost Per Acquisition (CPA) indicates that ads are gaining customers at a lesser expense, whereas a high Return on Investment (ROI) reflects a successful campaign.

- Amazon's AI-driven recommendation system and automated ad optimization highlight the effectiveness of data in providing highly tailored and efficient advertising.

- Advertisers who utilize analytics, machine learning, and ongoing testing will be optimally placed to connect with the appropriate audience at the ideal time with the correct message.

- Although numbers assist in honing strategy, captivating narratives, appealing visuals, and effective messaging are crucial for successful advertising.

Quiz

1. **What does CTR (Click-Through Rate) measure in an advertising campaign?**

   a. The total number of times an ad is shown

   b. The percentage of people who click on an ad after seeing it

   c. The total amount spent on an ad campaign

   d. The number of conversions from an ad

2. **If an ad campaign has 50,000 impressions and 1,000 clicks, what is its CTR?**

   a. 0.2%

   b. 2%

   c. 20%

   d. 5%

3. **Which of the following is the best measure of whether an ad is driving sales or sign-ups?**

   a. Impressions

   b. Click-Through Rate (CTR)

   c. Conversion Rate

   d. Cost Per Mille (CPM)

4. **What does Cost Per Acquisition (CPA) tell advertisers?**

   a. The total amount spent on an ad campaign

   b. How much is spent to acquire each customer

   c. The percentage of people who see an ad and click on it

   d. The cost for every 1,000 impressions

5. **A high CPA (Cost Per Acquisition) means:**
   a. You are getting customers at a low cost.
   b. Your ad campaign is very efficient.
   c. You are spending more money to get each customer.
   d. Your impressions are increasing.

6. **What is the formula for calculating Cost Per Click (CPC)?**
   a. Total Clicks ÷ Total Ad Spend
   b. Total Ad Spend ÷ Total Clicks
   c. Total Ad Spend ÷ Total Impressions
   d. Total Conversions ÷ Total Clicks

7. **What is the primary purpose of Google Analytics for advertisers?**
   a. To create social media ads
   b. To track website traffic and user behavior
   c. To design and edit ad creatives
   d. To monitor competitors' advertising strategies

8. **Why are UTM parameters useful in advertising?**
   a. They make ads more visually appealing.
   b. They track where website traffic is coming from.
   c. They help create better ad copy.
   d. They increase the CTR of an ad.

9. **Which of the following social media platforms provides built-in analytics for tracking ad performance?**
   a. Facebook
   b. Instagram
   c. Twitter
   d. All of the above

10. **A company runs two ad campaigns: one on Facebook and one on Instagram. They find that 70% of their traffic is coming from Instagram. What should they do?**
    a. Invest more in Instagram ads
    b. Stop advertising on social media
    c. Increase their CPC on Facebook
    d. Focus only on impressions

Answers

1 – b	2 – b	3 – c	4 – b	5 – c
6 – b	7 – b	8 – b	9 – d	10 – a

Case Study: Amazon - Data-Driven Advertising

Amazon's advertising effectiveness is strongly based on its data-driven strategy, allowing the company to enhance user experiences and boost conversion rates. Through detailed examination of user actions and the deployment of sophisticated recommendation systems, Amazon has established a standard in personalized marketing techniques.

This case study examines how Amazon's reliance on data, sophisticated recommendation systems, and AI-enhanced advertising techniques have transformed digital marketing, establishing a benchmark for personalized, high-performing, and perpetually refined ad experiences within the e-commerce sector.

Achievements Founded on Referrals

At the heart of Amazon's approach is its advanced recommendation system, which customizes product recommendations according to each user's interactions. This system uses item-to-item collaborative filtering, examining browsing habits, purchase records, and viewed items to create tailored recommendations.

This degree of customization not only enhances the shopping experience but also significantly boosts sales. Reports indicate that Amazon's recommendation system accounts for almost 35% of its total sales.

Strategies for Advertising Driven by Data

In addition to suggestions, Amazon utilizes extensive datasets to enhance its advertising strategies. Through monitoring user activity on its platform, Amazon acquires knowledge about consumer preferences, facilitating the development of targeted advertising campaigns. This data-driven strategy guarantees that ads are pertinent to users, thus boosting the chances of interaction and conversion.

For example, Amazon's ad platform provides features such as Sponsored Brands budget management that enables advertisers to establish performance-based guidelines. This system employs Amazon's first-party data and machine learning technology to enhance campaign effectiveness, guaranteeing that advertisements target the most pertinent audiences.

Enhancing User Interaction via A/B Testing

To improve its advertising efficiency, Amazon utilizes A/B testing techniques. By showcasing various ad versions to separate user groups, Amazon can evaluate which iterations produce the greatest engagement and conversion rates. This cyclical procedure facilitates the ongoing enhancement of promotional material, guaranteeing peak effectiveness.

For instance, Amazon's strategy for optimizing Sponsored Brands utilizes models that assess previous campaign results. If expenses are considered too high, bids are lowered; on the other hand, if potential is recognized, bids might be raised. Based on insights obtained from data, this adaptive modification guarantees that marketing initiatives are impactful and successful.

Machine Learning and Artificial Intelligence Integration

Amazon has demonstrated its dedication to innovation by incorporating machine learning and artificial intelligence into its advertising system. Through the examination of extensive data sets, these technologies allow Amazon to foresee consumer actions and customize advertisements accordingly. This forecasting ability guarantees that users are shown products they are most inclined to buy, thus enhancing conversion rates.

Additionally, Amazon's latest efforts, including the beta of the Retail Ad Service, enable outside online retailers to present contextually appropriate ads through Amazon's sophisticated machine learning algorithms. This service allows retailers to effortlessly merge into Amazon's current advertising network, enhancing the scope and impact of their marketing initiatives.

Main Insights:

- Amazon's recommendation system shows that tailored experiences result in higher sales.

- Amazon's commitment to continuous testing and enhancement ensures that every advertising dollar is spent effectively, boosting performance and reducing waste.

- Through automation, bid modifications, and predictive analytics, Amazon enhances ad performance with little human involvement.

- As Amazon broadens its advertising technology to outside retailers, the future of advertising is pivoting towards first-party data and platform-centric ad ecosystems.

Sources: (Arsenault, 2025; Roth, 2025; Amazon, 2024)

Exercise: Diagnosing and Fixing an Ad Campaign

A fitness apparel brand is running an Instagram ad campaign for its new running shoes. The campaign has high engagement but low conversions, and the marketing team wants to understand why.

Here's the campaign data:

Metric	Instagram Ad
Total Impressions	80,000
Total Clicks	4,800
Total Conversions	120
Total Ad Spend ($)	4,800
Revenue Generated ($)	12,000

1. *Calculate the CTR, conversion rate, CPC, CPA, and ROI.*

2. *Identify the campaign's strengths and weaknesses.*

3. *Explain why people might be clicking but not converting.*

4. *Recommend three improvements to boost conversions.*

CHAPTER 10

The Crystal Ball: Advertising in the Age of AI and Beyond

Key Learning Objectives

- How artificial intelligence is revolutionizing advertising
- Creating fully immersive experiences with VR & AR
- Rise of Influencer Marketing 2.0
- Developing marketing ideas designed for the future

The advertising market is rapidly evolving. Developments such as virtual reality (VR), augmented reality (AR), and artificial intelligence (AI) have developed from vague concepts to vital elements of current brand-consumer interaction. They deliver highly customized, engaging, and data-driven experiences. These developments enable marketers to go beyond conventional methods.

This chapter explores the significant transformations taking place in the advertising sector, emphasizing how AI improves campaign effectiveness. It helps you understand how VR and AR create deeper emotional connections and how influencer marketing is adapting to the need for genuineness. We will also explore innovative approaches that will help brands stay competitive in a constantly changing market.

10.1 The Advancement of AI in Advertising

The advertising sector is evolving due to artificial intelligence (AI). It plays a big role in allowing companies to deliver more customized experiences, improve ad effectiveness, and forecast consumer behavior more precisely. AI drives marketing progress by enhancing chatbots, automating advertising, and generating dynamic content. This has revolutionized the way companies connect with their target audiences.

10.1.1 Key Ways AI is Changing Advertising

We looked at how brands modify their marketing strategy through traditional tailoring in a previous chapter. The main methods used for this include purchase history analysis, consumer feedback, and demographic segmentation. These approaches are constrained by batch processing, manual data gathering, and a lack of real-time flexibility, even though they permit a certain amount of customization.

An advertising agency might, for instance, look at past campaign outcomes and divide audiences into main groups (for instance, "women aged 25-34 interested in fitness") and then create tailored email ads for each group. However, this batch-oriented approach suggests that client preferences may have changed by the time a campaign is launched.

In contrast, AI-driven tailoring offers instantaneous personalization, constantly analyzing vast amounts of real-time data and adjusting advertising content on the fly. Some examples include:

1. **Pinterest's AI-Powered Ad Targeting:** Unlike traditional agencies that create preset audience segments, Pinterest's Performance+ AI tool automatically adjusts ad placement based on real-time user behavior. AI identifies which users are most likely to engage and dynamically modifies targeting and bidding to optimize click-through rates and conversions (Singh, 2025).

2. **Yum Brands' AI-Powered Personalized Marketing:** While traditional marketers send generic promotional emails, Yum Brands (Taco Bell, KFC, Pizza Hut) analyzes customer purchase history and behavior in real time. AI customizes app notifications and loyalty rewards based on what a customer is most likely to buy at that moment, leading to double-digit increases in engagement (Graham, 2024).

Figure 10.1 provides an outline of some of the key ways that AI is impacting advertising today. Let us take a detailed look at these.

Figure 10.1 **The Impact of AI on Advertising**

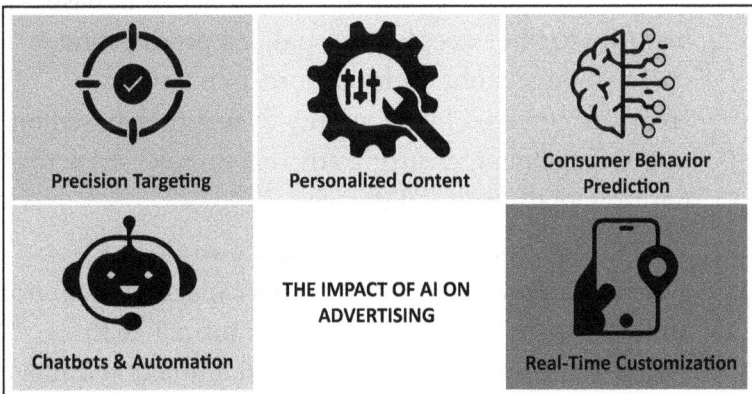

- Precision Targeting
- Personalized Content
- Consumer Behavior Prediction
- Chatbots & Automation
- THE IMPACT OF AI ON ADVERTISING
- Real-Time Customization

1. **Precision Targeting at Scale**

This technique uses AI algorithms to expedite the real-time acquisition and placement of digital ads. It improves return on investment (ROI) by analyzing vast amounts of data to identify the ideal audience, time, and platform for each ad. A few instances of this are:

- **The Economist's AI-Powered Effort:** Utilizing programmatic advertising, The Economist engaged with audiences who had not encountered its content before. This strategy resulted in over 650,000 new subscribers and an outstanding 10:1 ROI, achieved through customized ads based on online behaviors (Draycott, 2016)
- **Coca-Cola's Marketing Fueled by Data:** The brand skillfully orchestrated intricate worldwide campaigns with targeted accuracy by utilizing AI for automated ad purchasing (Marr, 2023).

2. **Tailoring Content to Individual Preferences**

AI is able to identify subtle patterns and microtrends in consumer behavior that a traditional agency would find difficult to identify in contrast to human analysis. Netflix, for instance, utilizes viewing and purchase histories to offer deeply personalized product and content suggestions. Furthermore, dynamic ad creatives powered by AI modify in real-time based on user engagement, ensuring ads remain relevant across multiple platforms and devices.

This automation improves efficiency while also generating ethical issues since AI's capacity to monitor and anticipate behaviors may seem intrusive. In contrast to conventional agencies that function under clear data collection agreements, AI can occasionally obscure the distinctions between personalization and invasion of privacy. Achieving a balance between personalization and consumer privacy continues to be a significant challenge in advertising driven by AI.

Some examples include:

- **Netflix's Recommendation Engine:** Influences 80% of the content viewed on the platform. By looking at viewing habits, AI recommends shows and movies to users and increases engagement (Medium, 2019).
- **Starbucks' DeepBrew AI System:** Starbucks leverages AI to personalize customer interactions, such as app suggestions and loyalty program deals, according to past purchases and user preferences (Hyperight, 2021).

3. Anticipating Consumer Behavior

Using AI-driven analytics, brands can understand consumer preferences, spot trends, and make informed decisions. This insight makes marketing campaigns and tactics more effective.

For instance:

- **Amazon:** According to Kopalle (2014), Amazon's Anticipatory Shipping algorithm anticipates what customers will purchase and distributes items to nearby warehouses in advance to speed up delivery times.
- **Sephora:** Sephora employs artificial intelligence (AI) to guide product recommendations that predict customer behavior based on previous purchases, hence increasing opportunities for cross-selling and upselling (Renascence, 2024).

4. Enhancing Customer Interaction

AI chatbots provide rapid support, similar to virtual assistants. They streamline the purchasing procedure and respond to your questions.

For instance, H&M's Kik Chatbots improve the shopping experience and simplify online buying. They guide customers in selecting outfits that suit their personal style, enhancing convenience and satisfaction (Redress Compliance, 2025).

5. Real-Time Ad Customization

Dynamic Creative Optimization (DCO) utilizes AI to modify ad creatives instantly according to factors like location, weather conditions, or user actions. Consequently, ads continue to be pertinent and interesting.

For example, Spotify's Dynamic Ads utilize AI to generate dynamic audio ads that adjust to users' listening patterns, the time of day, and weather conditions, improving the personalization of advertising experiences (Perez, 2021).

10.1.2 Ethical Considerations in AI Advertising

Although AI offers numerous benefits, it also poses ethical dilemmas:

1. **Data Privacy:** If customer information is not gathered and used in a transparent manner for tailored advertising, privacy violations may result.

2. **Algorithmic bias:** AI programs may inadvertently reinforce the prejudices found in their training data, which could result in unfair ad targeting results.

3. **Absence of Human Supervision:** Over-reliance on AI may result in automatic choices that ignore ethical factors, especially in delicate advertising efforts.

10.2 Creating Fully Immersive Experiences with VR & AR

The search by brands for new means of engaging audiences and creating memorable experiences continues to advance the boundaries of advertising.

With Virtual and Augmented Reality allowing consumers to touch, feel, and engage with products and brands in ways unimaginable just a decade ago, both are being hailed as go-to technologies where brands need to reimagine storytelling, flaunt their goods, and engage with audiences.

Though VR immerses customers in a virtual world completely via headsets such as Oculus Rift or HTC Vive, AR places digital information on the physical world using smartphones or AR glasses. Both these technologies make customers more interactive and emotional.

10.2.1. Product Visualization: Try Before You Buy

One of the most visible uses of AR in marketing is product visualization, whereby consumers are allowed to "try before they buy." This reduces uncertainty and increases confidence at the point of purchase.

L'Oréal virtual try-on application, equipped with AR capability, allows customers to try different makeup products virtually. This improves customer shopping experience and reduces product returns since customers can view their potential effects beforehand before buying (L'Oréal, n.d).

They bridge online shopping and the in-store browsing experience, giving brands an edge in e-commerce.

10.2.2. Storytelling Through Immersive Experiences

Apart from product demos, VR is revolutionizing brand storytelling by creating extremely engaging stories that form emotional connections with viewers.

An example is Volvo's VR campaign for its XC90 model, which offered a virtual test drive. This innovative approach engaged potential customers by providing a hands-on, memorable feel for the car without leaving their homes. Watch it in the Online Resources under Volvo XC90 Test Drive - Volvo Virtual Reality.

These experiences create lasting impressions because they don't just tell a story—they allow consumers to live it.

10.2.3. AR in Advertising Spaces: Beyond the Screen

AR is changing conventional advertising areas into vibrant, engaging experiences. Static billboards, magazine spreads, and even product wrappers can now be animated with captivating content.

For example, Pepsi's augmented reality bus shelter initiative in London astonished travelers with realistic images of alien attacks, robots, and exotic wildlife appearing on the streets. This surprising engagement not only drew attention but also went viral, highlighting AR's ability to generate exciting campaigns. Watch it in the Online Resources section under Pepsi MAX | Unbelievable Bus Shelter

10.2.4. Enhancing In-Store Experiences with AR & VR

In retail, AR and VR are improving the in-store experience by giving customers extra product info, virtual assistants, and personalized suggestions.

These technologies make the shopping experience more interactive, personalized, and efficient, so customers' satisfaction and loyalty to the brand increase.

10.2.5. Virtual Events and Global Brand Engagement

VR and AR go beyond product demos and retail. Organizations are using the technology for virtual events and experiences, overcoming geographical limits to reach people all over the world.

Though VR and AR have many benefits, there are some challenges, too. High-quality immersive content is expensive to develop, and not everyone has the required equipment, especially for VR. Privacy issues also come with AR apps that require permission to access personal information like location and camera.

Ethically, there is a fine line between immersive experiences and deceptive practices. As new technologies develop, companies need to make sure they respectfully and honestly enhance reality. Any immersive advertisement must be authentic in order to truly affect its audience.

Exercise 10.1: AI in Practice: Creating an
Intelligent Advertising Campaign

Select a brand or product that you prefer. Create an
AI-driven advertising campaign that utilizes predictive
analytics, chatbots, or tailored content.

- *Detail how AI will enhance targeting, engagement, and
  conversion rates.*

- *Reflect on possible ethical issues and how you would
  manage them.*

- *In what ways does AI improve your campaign relative
  to conventional approaches?*

- *What obstacles could emerge when adopting AI-based
  approaches?*

10.3 The Rise of Influencer Marketing 2.0

As time has passed, influencer marketing has advanced
from the celebrity endorsement sponsorship model's primal
version to a more universally recognized strategic form,
including ad placement and working with content creators
collaboratively. The emphasis of Influencer Marketing
2.0 has transitioned from basic promotional techniques
to encouraging authentic conversations and meaningful
collaborations between brands and content creators. This
transformation enhances it as a more reliable and effective
marketing approach by highlighting genuineness and
continuous engagement.

Unlike traditional influencer marketing, which is all about
surface-level promotion, this new approach is all about
building relationships between the brands, influencers, and
their audience.

The new-age buyer is very smart and can spot fake promotions easily. So, companies are moving away from shallow metrics like the number of followers, and are focusing on real connections.

This has given rise to micro-influencers, nano-influencers, and content creators who promote more authenticity in their interactions. Figure 10.2 below highlights some key points on influencer marketing.

Figure 10.2 Key Tenets of Influencer Marketing

Authenticity	Rise of Micro / Nano-Influencers	Influencer-Generated Content (IGC) as a Marketing Asset
Trust-driven, genuine influencer-brand relationships	Smaller audiences, deeper engagement	User-led marketing content for brands

10.3.1. The Shift Toward Authenticity

The digital realm has fostered a setting in which authenticity is not merely appreciated — it's anticipated. Viewers seek authentic content that aligns with their values, experiences, and hopes. This has prompted brands to collaborate with influencers who align with their values rather than just choose people with substantial follower counts.

10.3.2. Nano and Micro-Influencers

Micro-influencers with 10,000–100,000 followers and nano-influencers with fewer than 10,000 followers are beginning to receive more attention from businesses. They have very engaged, niche followers who look to them for advice and, therefore, higher conversion rates.

Nano-influencers are great for hyper-local marketing. Their small audience sees them as friends or peers, so their recommendations carry more weight. For example, local coffee shops, fitness studios, or boutique brands work with nano-influencers to target a specific demographic within their community without the big budget.

10.3.3 Content Created by Influencers (CCI) as a Marketing Resource

Another significant advancement in Influencer Marketing 2.0 is the tactical application of influencer-generated content (IGC) outside of social media postings. Brands now utilize influencer content for promotions, websites, email marketing, and even printed materials. This material seems more connected to audiences than conventional advertisements since it involves actual individuals recounting genuine experiences.

IGC delivers brands a continuous flow of original, genuine content that showcases the variety within their customer base, improving marketing strategies across various channels, which encompass:

1. **Enduring Collaborations Instead of Single Transactions:** In the past, influencer brand partnerships were limited to one-off collaborations, where an influencer would post about a product once. Influencer Marketing 2.0 is about

long-term partnerships that build stronger relationships and consistent messaging. Long-term partnerships allow influencers to seamlessly integrate products into their daily routine and show real use, not rehearsed promos. This helps brands build trust with audiences who value authenticity over advertising.

2. **TikTok and New Platforms:** TikTok changed influencer marketing by enabling anyone to create content. It thrives with genuine, unfiltered videos that demonstrate originality and sincerity, in contrast to Instagram's polished appearance. Remember Ocean Spray from Chapter 1? The video's raw appeal resonated with millions and led to a big jump in Ocean Spray sales and brand awareness, with no official sponsorship (The Guardian, 2020). This example shows the unpredictable nature of influencer marketing in the digital age. Brands need to be flexible and ready to join in with viral moments organically rather than forcing traditional marketing tactics.

3. **Influencer Promotion in B2B Settings:** Although influencer marketing is often associated with B2C industries, B2B companies are also using thought leaders and industry experts to boost their credibility. In B2B influencer marketing, the focus shifts from lifestyle influencers to experts who have deep knowledge and who impact business decisions.

10.3.4. Challenges in Influencer Marketing 2.0

Even with its development, influencer marketing faces difficulties. Transparency and openness are essential, as current regulations mandate that influencers must distinctly label sponsored content. Not complying can result in legal consequences and harm brand credibility.

Another difficulty is tackling influencer fraud, as phony followers and engagement statistics generate deceptive perceptions. Brands should thoroughly evaluate influencers, prioritizing genuine engagement metrics over mere superficial figures.

Lastly, preserving authenticity in a more commercialized influencer landscape can be challenging. An excess of sponsored content can drive audiences away, so it's essential for brands to choose influencers who truly reflect their values.

Exercise 10.2: VR/AR Ad Concept

Imagine you're creating an ad for a travel agency, fashion brand, or tech company.

1. *Develop an idea for an AR or VR experience that engages consumers beyond traditional ads.*

2. *Describe the user journey*

3. *Identify the key message the immersive experience will convey.*

10.4 Staying Ahead: Planning for the Future of Advertising

With technology advancing and consumer behavior changing, cultural patterns are transformed, and so too is the future of advertising. Brands need to be able to keep up with what is current, as well as forecast what will be next, if they are going to make it. Being ahead in advertising is not just about embracing new technology but also about promoting creativity, embracing change, and maintaining real connections. Some of the things to keep in mind are:

1. **The Importance of Adaptability in Advertising**

   In a time when change is the sole certainty, flexibility is a crucial competitive edge. Brands that withstand change run the risk of obsolescence, whereas those that adopt innovation can create fresh market prospects. For example, businesses such as Netflix shifted from DVD rentals to streaming, not merely as a business strategy but by reshaping how content is consumed and how advertising works in that arena.

   Key Takeaways:

   - Adopt New Technologies: Don't merely respond to trends; test out AI-based content generation, virtual reality experiences, or voice-responsive marketing prior to their widespread adoption.

   - Analytics-Based Adaptability: Employ live data insights to adjust campaigns rapidly according to audience responses. Services such as Spotify accomplish this well by tailoring their highly personalized advertisements according to user listening behaviors.

2. **The Growth of Predictive Analytics**

   Organizations' ability to predict trends, analyze customer behavior, and optimize advertising is being transformed by predictive analytics. Advertisers can now predict what people want before they even realize it, rather than relying solely on historical data.

   For example, the recommendation system at Amazon uses predictive algorithms to suggest products, which considerably boosts conversion rates. Technology in advertising helps firms deliver more relevant information, minimize ad fatigue, and serve highly targeted content.

Uses in Marketing:

- Personalized Dynamic Advertising: Customizing messages according to anticipated actions.
- Campaign Enhancement: Modifying expenditure instantly to increase ROI.
- Trend Prediction: Recognizing changes in consumer preferences to maintain cultural relevance.

3. Ethical Marketing in the Digital Era

Growing advertising technology creates more ethical problems. All of these have been caused by algorithmic bias, data privacy, and the psychological consequences of highly customized ads. Businesses need to strike a balance between personalization and respect for customer autonomy.

An instance of this being mishandled happened in December 2024 when Spotify's yearly "Wrapped" function, which relied heavily on generative AI, encountered significant criticism. Users expressed dissatisfaction that earlier versions were missing the tailored, unique features and detailed statistics. Numerous individuals felt let down by the AI-created content, as they perceived it to be lacking a personal touch and engaging quality. (Di Placido, 2024).

This situation highlights the delicate equilibrium companies must maintain when integrating AI into user interfaces. An overreliance on AI could weaken user trust, especially if it diminishes the human aspect that users value. The backlash against Spotify Wrapped 2024 highlights the risks of substituting human creativity with artificial intelligence in user-interactive programs. (Gotfredson, 2024).

Strategies for Resilience in the Future:

- Clear Data Practices: Provide transparency regarding the collection and usage of consumer data.
- Accountable AI Implementation: Guarantee that algorithms do not perpetuate damaging stereotypes or biases.
- Genuine Storytelling: Foster trust via authentic, value-centered tales.

4. The Development of Consumer Anticipations

Contemporary consumers do not simply receive advertisements; they engage actively in brand stories. For instance, Nike's "Dream Crazy" campaign with Colin Kaepernick struck a chord since it matched the brand's principles, even with mixed responses.

What Consumers Anticipate Going Forward:

- Purpose-Focused Brands: Businesses that represent ideals beyond mere earnings.
- Engaging Experiences: Mutual interaction via social media, augmented reality, and real-time content.
- Sustainability and Social Influence: Environmentally conscious methods and true corporate accountability.

5. Readying for the Unforeseen

With AI, VR, and influencer marketing shaping the landscape today, the future will bring technologies and platforms we can't even imagine yet. Future-proofing isn't anticipating all changes, it's having a base of flexibility, innovation, and ongoing education.

Tips to be Ready for the Future:

- Have your teams trained up to speed on new technologies and marketing strategies.
- Allow for trial and error, even if it means some failures.
- Great ideas often come from unexpected places— look outside marketing for inspiration.

In Conclusion

Preparing for the future of advertising is about cultivating a mindset that welcomes change. Brands that succeed will be those that prioritize ethical practices, embrace technological advancements, and remain deeply connected to their audience's evolving needs.

Chapter Summary

- Artificial Intelligence (AI) enhances marketing through a high level of personalization.

- Virtual Reality (VR) and Augmented Reality (AR) offer engaging, immersive experiences that allow consumers to connect with brands in dynamic environments.

- Influencer marketing focuses on authenticity, long-lasting partnerships, and micro-influencers who serve highly engaged niche audiences.

- To stay competitive, brands need to embrace new technologies and foster a culture of continual innovation.

- As technology advances swiftly, brands that stay adaptable, try out new tools, and emphasize genuine consumer relationships.

Quiz

1. **How is AI transforming the advertising industry?**
   a. By eliminating the need for creative teams
   b. By automating ad creation without any human input
   c. By providing data-driven insights and enabling personalized marketing
   d. By reducing the number of ads, companies can produce

2. **Which IBM product played a key role in AI-driven advertising campaigns?**
   a. Red Hat
   b. Watson
   c. Deep Blue
   d. Cloud Pak

3. **In IBM's AI-driven advertising strategies, AI is used primarily to:**
   a. Replace human marketers
   b. Create art without human oversight
   c. Analyze consumer data to optimize campaigns and enhance decision-making
   d. Generate advertisements without any creative input from humans

4. **Which of the following is a key advantage of AI in advertising?**
   a. AI completely removes the need for creativity.
   b. AI replaces the need for marketing teams.
   c. AI reduces the cost of products.
   d. AI helps analyze large data sets to optimize campaigns.

5. **In influencer marketing 2.0, brands focus on:**
   a. Building authentic connections with niche audiences
   b. Working only with celebrities
   c. Ignoring data analytics in favor of emotions
   d. Relying solely on paid ads for promotion

6. **Which technology creates fully immersive advertising experiences?**
   a. Virtual Reality (VR) and Augmented Reality (AR)
   b. Blockchain
   c. Cloud Computing
   d. Cryptocurrency

7. **What does AR stand for in advertising technology?**
   a. Automatic Recognition
   b. Augmented Reality
   c. Advanced Research
   d. Artificial Response

8. **What was the goal of IBM's "Outthink" campaign?**
   a. To promote traditional marketing strategies
   b. To showcase how businesses can outthink competitors using AI
   c. To sell physical products
   d. To create viral social media memes

9. **One key ethical concern in AI-driven advertising is:**
   a. High production costs
   b. Too much human creativity
   c. Lack of automation
   d. Data privacy and transparency

10. **Which of the following best describes Virtual Reality (VR) in advertising?**

   a. A new social media platform
   b. A way to print 3D ads
   c. A technology that transports users into a simulated, interactive environment
   d. A traditional marketing tactic

Answers

1 – c	2 – b	3 – c	4 – c	5 – d
6 – a	7 – b	8 – b	9 – d	10 – c

Case Study: IBM — Pioneering the Future of Advertising with AI

IBM has always been at the forefront of innovation, and its marketing approach reflects that. IBM has transformed brand-audience interaction with data-driven insights, responsible storytelling, and artificial intelligence (AI).

The Rise of IBM Watson in Advertising

At the heart of IBM's marketing approach is IBM Watson, a sophisticated AI system that can learn from big data, understand natural language, and make predictions. IBM marketed Watson not just as a product but also as a technology that could change multiple industries.

A big campaign was "IBM Watson: Outthink", to show how Watson could help businesses outthink their competition. The campaign showed Watson analyzing complex data faster than a person, revealing insights that lead to better decisions.

Essential Elements of the Campaign:

- **Storytelling Through Tangible Results:** IBM showed practical uses of Watson, including helping doctors diagnose rare diseases, improve weather forecasts, and even create film trailers.
- **Data-Driven Creativity:** Watson used audience data to enhance ads and deliver tailored and relevant messaging across channels.
- **Multi-Channel Approach:** The campaign ran across TV, online, print, and in-person events, always enhancing the IBM message.

Ethical Considerations of AI-Driven Advertising

Despite being creative, IBM's AI advertising raised big questions about data protection, transparency, and how AI affects human behaviour. IBM tackled these issues by:

- **AI Ethics:** IBM developed policies that saw AI as an addition to human intelligence rather than a replacement for it.
- **Transparency:** They won the audience's trust by being open and honest about the usage of AI in their commercials.

Results and Impact

IBM's future-focused advertising strategy delivered:

- **Brand Perception:** IBM moved from being seen as a traditional tech company to a leader in AI innovation.
- **Business Growth:** The Watson campaign drove enterprise adoption of AI solutions across industries.
- **Thought Leadership:** IBM positioned itself as the authority on ethical AI, influencing industry standards for responsible technology.

Key Takeaways:

1. IBM's success can be credited to its ability to blend innovative technology with emotionally engaging stories.
2. Maintaining consumer trust in the AI era requires ethical considerations; they are not optional.

IBM's advertising campaigns demonstrate how AI-driven insights and human creativity are combined for optimum impact in the future of advertising.

Source: (IBM, 2016)

Exercise: "Future-Ready" Ad Blueprint

Design a blueprint for an ad campaign that integrates AI, immersive technology, and ethical practices.

Your blueprint should include:

1. *Target audience*
2. *Key message*
3. *Technology integration (AI, VR, AR)*
4. *Ethical considerations*
5. *Metrics for success*

Further Learning

Links also available in Online Resources

1. **Volvo XC90 Test Drive - Volvo Virtual Reality**
   http://bit.ly/4mbVpZ3
2. **Pepsi MAX | Unbelievable Bus Shelter**
   http://bit.ly/4nYo5GR

CASE STUDY 1: How Kia Australia Used Integrated Brand Marketing to Achieve Record Sales

In 2024, Kia Australia stood at a fork in the road. The Australian motor vehicle industry was extremely competitive, with Toyota, Ford, and Mazda out in front. These were all established brands, with a good reputation for reliability, innovation, and high customer loyalty. Kia was a good brand in its value-for-money and cost-efficient reputation but behind its rivals in perceived quality and desirability.

In order to continue growing and remain a leader, Kia must create an integrated, brand-focused experience outside of ads. This demanded a multi-faceted marketing campaign of advertising, public relations, strategic partnerships, and consumer engagement to develop more emotional relationships with consumers.

Advertising Strategy

The company leveraged three pillars of integrated marketing relating to brand messaging, deliberate sponsorship alignment, and storytelling:

1. **Single brand messaging through all channels**

   Kia turned its focus away from isolated campaigns to ensure that every point of engagement with a (potential) customer, be it through an advertisement, public relations event, or dealership transmitted the same brand values of reliability, innovation, and premium quality.

Kia's television commercials and internet commercials remapped Kia as a progressive, future-facing brand. Its Electric Vehicle (EV) commercials, for instance, stressed Kia's commitment to sustainability, aligning the brand with global environmental movements.

The brand had a presence on social media as well, engaging with people through interactive storytelling, video, and live experience. Unlike some of their rivals who uploaded product-focused posts, Kia's posts were interwoven with factory backstories, driver stories, and brand vision statements to humanize the brand.

2. Leverage strategic sponsorships for brand prestige

Kia took its long tradition of association with the Australian Open tennis tournament to new levels by supplementing its logo placement with on-court branding, immersive digital experiences, and influencer collaborations. The brand's activation spaces allowed fans to experience Kia's new models through immersive VR, bringing its reputation for high performance and excellence to life in a tangible way. In so doing, it was able to change the consumer's view of the business from a bargain brand option to an aspirational buying choice.

3. Stand out from competitors through storytelling

The two largest product launches in 2024 by Kia—the Tasman Ute, as well as its growing battery-electric range—exploited tale-structured advertising.

The launch of the Tasman Ute

Kia launched the Tasman Ute in 2024, a new model specifically engineered to withstand the rigors of the Australian climate. The campaign was created to appeal to local drivers, emphasizing off-road capability, ruggedness, and outdoor lifestyle appeal. To create authenticity, Kia collaborated with well-known Australian sports figures and car writers, who tested the vehicle in real-world conditions (Skinner, 2025).

The EV Campaign

Instead of focusing entirely on specifications and features, Kia's EV ads tuned into lifestyle changes among consumers, showing how electric vehicles easily fit into modern, sustainable living.

The firm also tapped into experiential online moments, allowing prospective buyers to customize EV models in virtual dealerships before they set foot in a store.

Results: Measurable Business and Brand Impact

Let's see how Kia Australia's integrated brand marketing strategy delivered impressive results:

Record sales and market expansion: Kia achieved over 80,000 car sales in Australia in 2024, its record-breaking sales year, and solidified its position as Australia's fourth-largest producer.

Improved brand perception: Post-campaign brand tracking revealed a 15% increase in positive favorability towards the brand, with Kia being seen as more innovative, premium, and consumer-focused than ever.

Boosted customer engagement: Kia's sports sponsorships and interactive digital experiences raised social engagement by 35%, demonstrating that integrated marketing generates not just awareness, but also useful brand interactions.

EV and Tasman Ute success: The pre-launch campaigns drove strong pre-orders, demonstrating once again that product storytelling and local market alignment drive purchasing intent.

Key Takeaways

- A thriving brand is created through consistency, narrative, and well-planned brand interactions.
- Messages must remain uniform throughout all customer engagements, from advertisements to social media updates to the ambiance in retail locations.
- Sponsorships must be used strategically, to elevate the brand's value and trigger meaningful experiences.
- Effective storytelling creates brand loyalty in the long term when compared to product specifications.

Sources: (Car Expert & Wong, 2025); (MI-3, 2025); (TechDriveplay & Skinner, 2025); (Campaign Brief & Green, 2025).

References:

1. Car Expert & Wong, J.(2025, January 10). *Kia Australia has record 2024, cracks 80,000 annual sales.* Retrieved February 20, 2025, from https://www.carexpert.com.au/car-news/kia-australia-has-record-2024-cracks-80000-annual-sales

2. MI-3.(2025, January 14). *Kia Australia unleashes zombie apocalypse in new EV campaign.* Retrieved February 20, 2025, from https://www.mi-3.com.au/14-01-2025/

kia-australia-unleashes-zombie-apocalypse-new-ev-campaign

3. TechDriveplay & Skinner, Z.(2025, February 28). *Kia Australia Reveals Highly Anticipated Tasman Ute Campaign.* Retrieved March 2, 2025, from https://techdriveplay.com/2025/02/28/kia-australia-reveals-highly-anticipated-tasman-ute-campaign/

4. Campaign Brief & Green, R.(2025, January 13). *KIA expands presence at the Australian Open with Four Technology focused Experential Activations.* Retrieved March 2, 2025, from https://campaignbrief.com/kia-expands-presence-at-the-australian-open-with-four-technology-focused-experiential-activations/

CASE STUDY 2: Doritos—Reviving "Crash the Super Bowl" to Engage Audiences

In 2025, Doritos needed to resurrect its brand relevance by reviving its successful "Crash the Super Bowl" promotion, a winning consumer-created program that had been absent for ten years. Debuted in 2006, the program challenged consumers to develop their own Doritos commercials, with the winner having its ad broadcast during the Super Bowl.

This move democratized marketing as well as sparked intense consumer passion. Rebooting the campaign, Doritos wanted to use nostalgia while using User-Generated Content (UGC) to drive buzz in the weeks leading up to Super Bowl LIX.

Advertising Strategy

Doritos' advertising approach had three pillars:

1. **User-Generated Content (UGC) promotion**

   By asking fans to produce their own 30-second commercials, Doritos transformed consumers into creators, building ownership and personal connection to the brand. This generated plenty of diverse content while allowing Doritos to take advantage of the creativity of its audience's unique points of view.

2. **Nostalgia marketing**

   Re-running the "Crash the Super Bowl" campaign engaged loyal, long-time consumers who remembered the original campaign. Thus, connecting past and present brand experiences. The nostalgia factor was meant to remind and bring back positive memories and re-engage consumers who had participated in or enjoyed the campaign in its earlier forms.

3. **Digital engagement and voting mechanism**

   For maximum participation and engagement, Doritos designed a dedicated website, "doritoscrash.com," for customers to upload their videos and vote for the top entries. This interactive website made content submission more convenient and also encouraged community building through voting, commenting, and sharing on social media.

Executing a Multi-Phase Campaign Rollout

Here's how the brand captivated audiences and generated buzz leading up to the big game:

Phase 1: Campaign announcement and promotion

Doritos began by launching a series of teaser advertisements and social media posts, building anticipation and inciting followers to share. The brand utilized its principal channels as well as collaboration with influencers for the purpose of disseminating and ensuring widespread exposure.

Phase 2: Submission period

Members were given a set time frame to create and submit their commercials. Doritos provided parameters for brand consistency but encouraged creativity and originality. The special site was the central point for submissions, with friendly features to make it easy.

Phase 3: Public voting and engagement

When submissions closed, all the entries were posted on the site for public viewing and voting. Incentives were offered by Doritos in the way of prizes to the voters in the form of limited-edition merchandise and a chance to win Super Bowl tickets, thereby promoting participation.

Phase 4: Winner announcement and Super Bowl airing

The most popular ad, as voted by people, was announced the winner and aired during the Super Bowl, giving the creator national exposure and affirming Doritos' commitment to its consumers.

Campaign Outcomes

The campaign yielded significant outcomes as follows:

1. **Surge in user participation**

   The campaign generated thousands of submissions, demonstrating the passion and creativity of Doritos fans. The influx of content not only amplified the brand's marketing assets but also demonstrated the strength of UGC in creating a community.

2. **Enhanced digital footprint**

   The dedicated website attracted millions of visitors, with users actively engaging in viewing, voting, and sharing content. This digital buzz translated to increased brand visibility across social media platforms, amplifying Doritos' reach.

3. **Positive brand sentiment**

   By directly engaging the consumers through its Super Bowl ads, Doritos made a bold statement about itself as a brand that values and respects its consumers. This heightened brand affinity and positivity because consumers felt appreciated and respected.

4. **Media coverage and publicity**

   The campaign's novel method was picked up by many media sources, providing free publicity and debate over Doritos' creative marketing initiative.

Key Takeaways

Doritos' "Crash the Super Bowl" campaign demonstrates the strength of immersing consumers in the brand narrative through:

- **Embracing user-generated content:** UGC not only offers variation in marketing content but also creates a community between the brand and consumers. This increases levels of commitment.

- **Reaching into the past:** Recycling successful old campaigns has the potential to revive positive sentiments and dropped consumers, and attract new ones through established precedent.

- **Encouraging active participation:** Engaging campaigns that invite consumers to participate can encourage greater levels of engagement since individuals are more likely to endorse and share material that interests them.

- **Utilizing digital channels:** Dedicated digital channels for voting and submissions can consolidate involvement, and consumers can readily involve themselves in the campaign and share content.

By resurrecting a beloved promotion and giving its consumers creative power, Doritos not only did its fans justice but also demonstrated the staying power of user-generated content and nostalgia in today's advertising.

Source: (Website Builder Expert & Choules, 2025 and Socially Powerful, 2025)

References:

1. Socially Powerful (2025, January 16). *The 2025 Marketing Campaigns That Have Already Won The Year.* Retrieved February 20, 2025, from https://sociallypowerful.com/post/2025-marketing-campaigns

2. Website Builder Expert & Choules, H.(2025, January 28). *These Were the 4 Best Marketing Campaigns in January 2025.* Retrieved February 20, 2025, from https://www.websitebuilderexpert.com/news/best-marketing-campaigns-january-2025/

Glossary

A/B Testing: An advertising method where two versions of an ad are tested to determine which one performs better.

Ad Transparency: A principle that requires brands to clearly disclose ad sponsorships, pricing, and terms so consumers can make informed decisions.

Advertising: A form of communication used by brands, businesses, and organizations to promote products, services, or ideas.

AIDA Model (Attention, Interest, Desire, Action): A classic copywriting formula that guides the structure of ad messaging to attract attention, build interest, create desire, and drive action.

Artificial Intelligence (AI) in Advertising: Utilizing machine learning algorithms to analyze consumer data, personalize ads, and automate campaign management. This improves efficiency and targeting accuracy.

Attribution Modeling: A method for identifying which touchpoints in the customer journey contribute to a conversion, helping marketers allocate budget efficiently.

Audience Segmentation: Dividing a large audience into smaller, more defined groups based on characteristics like demographics, behavior, and interests for more precise advertising.

Augmented Reality (AR) in Ads: Interactive experiences where digital elements overlay the real world, such as virtual try-ons for clothing and furniture previews in home settings.

Authority Bias: A tendency of consumers to trust and follow advice from figures of authority, such as industry experts, celebrities, or professionals in white lab coats in advertisements.

Bandwagon Effect: The tendency to adopt a trend or behavior because others are doing it.

Behavioral Targeting: A strategy that uses a person's online activity, such as search history, website visits, and past purchases, to serve relevant ads.

Billboards: Large outdoor ads placed in high-traffic areas to capture attention quickly

Blockchain in Advertising: A decentralized system that increases transparency in digital advertising, reducing fraud and ensuring advertisers pay for genuine engagement rather than bots.

Bounce Rate: The percentage of visitors who leave a website without taking action. This helps evaluate landing page effectiveness.

Brand Accountability: The expectation that brands own up to mistakes, correct misleading campaigns, and align their advertising with ethical values.

Brand Consistency: Maintaining a uniform look, feel, and tone across all platforms to build trust and recognition among consumers.

Brand Equity: The perceived value and strength of a brand in the market which impact its pricing power, consumer trust, and overall reputation.

Brand Guidelines: A set of rules and standards that define how a brand should be represented visually and verbally across different channels and marketing materials.

Brand Identity: The visual, verbal, and emotional elements that define how a brand presents itself to the world, including logos, colors, fonts, and messaging.

Brand Loyalty: The degree to which consumers repeatedly choose a brand over competitors, driven by positive experiences and strong emotional connections.

Brand Positioning: How a brand differentiates itself in the minds of consumers, emphasizing unique values, target audience, and competitive advantage.

Brand Recognition: The ability of consumers to identify a brand based on visual cues like its logo, slogan, or packaging, even without seeing its name.

Brand Voice: The consistent tone, language, and style a brand uses in its messaging, reflecting its personality and values.

Business-to-Business Marketing (B2B Marketing): Advertising targeted at businesses rather than individual consumers.

Business-to-Consumer Marketing (B2C): Marketing aimed at individual consumers.

Call to Action (CTA): A prompt in an ad that encourages immediate action.

Case Study Marketing: Using real-world examples to understand how brands succeed or fail in cultural advertising.

Cause-Related Advertising: Advertising that ties a brand to a social cause or movement, such as climate action, gender equality, or ethical sourcing.

Cause-Washing: A tactic where brands pretend to support social causes for profit, without taking meaningful action.

Clarity in Messaging: A copywriting principle that ensures ad messages are simple, easy to understand, and free of unnecessary jargon to maximize impact.

Clickbait: A misleading or exaggerated headline designed to attract clicks. It is often used to increase engagement but can harm credibility.

Click-Through Rate (CTR): A percentage that shows how many users clicked on an ad after seeing it, indicating ad engagement and effectiveness.

Cognitive Bias: A mental shortcut that influences how people perceive information and make decisions.

Color Psychology: The study of how colors influence perception and emotions. It is often used in branding to evoke specific feelings.

Consumer Protection Laws: Legal frameworks designed to protect consumers from misleading ads, ensuring fair competition and ethical business practices

Conversational Marketing: AI-powered chatbots, voice assistants, and messaging apps that provide personalized, real-time interactions between brands and consumers.

Conversion Rate: The percentage of users who complete a desired action after clicking an ad.

Conversion Rate Optimization (CRO): The process of refining a website or landing page to increase the percentage of visitors who complete a desired action.

Cost Per Acquisition (CPA): The total cost required to convert a user into a customer. It helps advertisers gauge campaign efficiency.

Cost Per Click (CPC): The amount an advertiser pays for each click on their ad.

Cost Per Mille (CPM): The cost of reaching 1,000 viewers in an advertising campaign. It is commonly used in brand awareness strategies.

Cross-Cultural Marketing: Developing advertising campaigns that appeal to multiple cultural groups by understanding linguistic, visual, and societal differences.

Cultural Backlash: A negative response from consumers when a brand misunderstands or disrespects cultural values, often leading to PR crises and brand reputation damage.

Cultural Sensitivity: The practice of understanding and respecting cultural differences to create marketing messages that resonate positively across different audiences.

Cultural Translation: Ensuring that advertising captures the intended meaning and emotional impact.

Curiosity Gap: A strategy where ad copy teases information to create curiosity, compelling readers to engage further.

Customer Lifetime Value (CLV): A prediction of how much revenue a customer will generate over their lifetime with a brand. It helps businesses determine long-term profitability.

Customer Persona: A detailed profile representing an ideal customer, including their pain points, habits, and motivations. It helps brands create more relatable marketing messages.

Dark Patterns in Marketing: Deceptive design techniques that trick users into actions they might not take voluntarily, such as forced subscriptions, hidden fees, or misleading opt-ins.

Data Privacy in Advertising: The ethical responsibility of brands to protect user data and ensure compliance with laws like GDPR (General Data Protection Regulation) and CCPA (California Consumer Privacy Act).

Data-Driven Decision Making: Using real-time insights and analytics to optimize advertising strategies, ensuring campaigns are efficient and cost-effective.

Decoy Effect: A pricing strategy where a third option is introduced to make one of the first two options seem more attractive, thus influencing purchase decisions.

Demographic Targeting: A method of delivering ads based on specific population characteristics such as age, gender, income, education, and occupation.

Digital and Global Integration: The AI-driven interconnectedness of advertising across cultures that requires brands to balance local relevance with global appeal.

Digital Advertising: The use of internet-based platforms such as social media, websites, and search engines to display advertisements.

Direct Response Advertising: Ads designed to trigger an instant consumer action, like signing up or purchasing.

Display Advertising: Graphical ads such as banners, pop-ups, and video ads that appear on websites, mobile apps, and digital platforms.

Emotional Appeal: A persuasion technique that evokes emotions such as excitement, fear, nostalgia, or happiness to connect with consumers and drive action.

Emotional Hook: A powerful emotional appeal used in advertising copy to resonate with consumers and create a lasting impression.

Engagement Rate: A metric that tracks likes, shares, comments, and interactions on social media ads to measure audience participation.

Ethical Advertising: The practice of creating truthful, transparent, and responsible campaigns that do not mislead, manipulate, or exploit consumers.

Ethical AI in Advertising: The responsible use of AI-powered marketing tools to avoid bias, misinformation, and unethical targeting.

Ethnocentrism: A bias where brands assume one cultural perspective is superior, leading to tone-deaf messaging or offensive branding missteps.

Exclusivity Appeal: A marketing approach where products are framed as elite, premium, or only available to a select group, making consumers desire them more.

Fair Competition: Ensuring that brands market their products honestly and do not engage in false comparisons, smear campaigns, or misleading competitor claims.

False Advertising: Misleading consumers by making deceptive claims about a product or service.

Fear of Missing Out (FOMO): A psychological trigger where consumers fear missing an opportunity, often used in marketing through limited-time offers and exclusivity tactics.

First-Party Data: Data collected directly from consumers by a brand, providing high-quality insights without third-party involvement.

Generational Marketing: Targeting consumers based on their generational preferences and behaviors, such as Baby Boomers valuing reliability, and Gen Zs favoring inclusivity and activism.

Geotargeting: A technique that serves ads to users based on their geographic location.

Global Branding: A branding strategy where a company maintains a unified identity and message across different countries while allowing for localized adaptations to fit cultural expectations.

Greenwashing: A marketing strategy where brands falsely present themselves as environmentally friendly to appeal to eco-conscious consumers.

Headline: The first and most prominent line of text in an ad, designed to grab attention and entice the reader to continue engaging with the content.

High-Converting Ad Copy: Text that drives a strong response and maximizes engagement, often refined through A/B testing and data analysis.

Hyper-Personalization: AI-driven real-time customization of ads based on a user's past behavior, interests, and online interactions to increase relevance and engagement.

Impressions: The number of times an ad is displayed on a screen,

Impulse Buy: An unplanned purchase that is triggered by emotions, visual cues, or strategic product placement.

Inclusive Advertising: The practice of representing diverse identities, backgrounds, and communities in advertising campaigns to reflect modern societal values.

Influencer Ethics: The responsibility of social media influencers to disclose sponsored content, ensuring transparency in product endorsements.

Influencer Marketing: A modern advertising tactic where brands partner with social media influencers or celebrities to promote products to their engaged followers, creating authentic endorsements and brand credibility.

Influencer Marketing: A strategy where brands partner with social media influencers or content creators to promote their products, leveraging the influencer's audience trust.

Influencer-Led AI Avatars: Virtual influencers and AI-generated brand ambassadors that engage with audiences and promote products without human involvement, expanding influencer marketing to digital-only personas.

Interactive & Gamified Ads: Advertising formats that encourage user participation, such as playable ads, branded games, and interactive quizzes to boost engagement and brand recall.

Jingles: Short, catchy tunes. They are used in advertisements to make a brand or product more memorable.

Key Performance Indicators (KPIs): Quantifiable metrics used to measure the effectiveness of advertising campaigns

Lead Generation: The process of attracting and converting potential customers into leads. It is often done through forms, email marketing, and gated content.

Limited-Time Offers: A strategy that creates urgency and fast decision-making by restricting how long a product or deal is available.

Localization: Adapting advertising content to fit the preferences, customs, and behaviors of a specific market.

Logo Design: A visual symbol representing a brand that often combines icons, typography, and color schemes to create instant brand recognition.

Lookalike Audience: A group of people who share similar characteristics and behaviors with an existing customer base.

Loss Aversion: A cognitive bias where people fear losing something more than they value gaining something new.

Manipulation: Distorting facts or playing on fears to mislead.

Mass Media: Communication channels that reach large audiences simultaneously, including television, radio, newspapers, and digital platforms.

Metaverse Advertising: Marketing strategies designed for virtual worlds, digital stores, and branded in-game experiences.

Native Advertising: A form of advertising that blends in with the surrounding content, making it appear more organic.

Nudging: A subtle marketing technique that guides consumer choices without them realizing it.

Pay-Per-Click (PPC) Advertising: An online ad model where advertisers pay only when users click their ads.

Personal Branding: The process of individuals crafting their own professional image using consistent messaging, design, and reputation-building strategies.

Persuasion: Using logical, emotional, and ethical appeals to influence decisions.

Persuasive Copywriting: A writing style that focuses on convincing the audience to take action through strategic wording, psychological triggers, and emotional appeal.

Power Words: Words that evoke emotion or urgency to make advertising copy more persuasive.

Predictive Analytics: The use of AI and machine learning to analyze past consumer behavior and predict future purchasing decisions.

Privacy-First Marketing: A shift toward consumer data protection, where brands must comply with GDPR, CCPA, and other privacy laws while still delivering effective advertising.

Product Placement: A form of advertising where brands pay to have their products featured in movies, TV shows, or online content, creating subtle yet powerful brand exposure.

Programmatic Advertising: An automated method of buying and placing ads in real-time, using AI and data to target the right audience at the right time.

Real-Time Bidding (RTB): An automated auction process where ad placements are bought and sold in real-time whenever a user loads a webpage.

Rebranding: The process of changing a brand's identity, messaging, or design to refresh its image and adapt to market trends.

Reciprocity Principle: People feel compelled to return a favor after receiving something first. Marketers use this through free samples, trials, and special gifts.

Regulatory Compliance: Laws and policies that govern fair advertising, such as the Federal Trade Commission (FTC) guidelines on misleading claims and the Advertising Standards Authority (ASA) regulations.

Retargeting (Remarketing): Ads shown to users who previously visited a website but didn't convert, encouraging them to return and complete the desired action.

Retargeting Metrics: Performance indicators that track how many past visitors return to complete an action after seeing a retargeting ad.

Return on Investment (ROI): A measure of how much revenue an advertising campaign generates compared to the cost of running it.

Scarcity Marketing: A tactic where brands limit the availability of a product to increase its perceived value, such as "Only 2 left in stock!" notifications.

Search Engine Marketing (SEM): A strategy that involves paid ads on search engines like Google and Bing to drive traffic to websites based on specific keyword searches.

Search Engine Optimization (SEO): A process of optimizing content and websites to rank higher on search engine results without paying for ads.

Shoppable Ads: Advertisements that allow consumers to purchase products directly within the ad experience. They're commonly used on Instagram, TikTok, and Pinterest.

Slogans: Short, memorable phrases that capture the essence of a brand or product.

Social Justice Marketing: A strategy where brands align with societal issues to engage with socially conscious consumers.

Social Media Advertising: Paid promotions on platforms such as Facebook, Instagram, TikTok, LinkedIn, and Twitter (X). This allows businesses to target users based on behavior, interests, and demographics.

Social Proof: A psychological phenomenon where people look to others to determine what is right or valuable.

Social Proof in Copy: The inclusion of testimonials, case studies, or user-generated content to build trust and credibility.

Status Symbol Branding: Positioning a product as a symbol of wealth, power, or success, making it more desirable to consumers.

Storytelling in Branding: Using narratives and emotional appeal to create deeper connections between a brand and its audience.

Symbolism: The use of icons, colors, and imagery that carry cultural meaning and significance.

Target Audience: The specific group of people that an advertisement is designed to reach. It is defined by factors like age, gender, location, interests, and purchasing behavior.

Targeted Advertising: The practice of using consumer data to deliver personalized ads.

The Cookieless Future: An anticipated norm where advertisers must rely on first-party data, contextual targeting, and privacy-compliant strategies for consumer engagement.

Typography in Branding: The choice of fonts and text styles contributing to a brand's personality and readability, ensuring cohesive messaging across platforms.

Urgency & Scarcity Tactics: A marketing technique that uses time-sensitive language to drive fast decision-making.

User-Generated Content (UGC): Content created by consumers or fans, such as reviews, testimonials, or social media posts, that is often used to build brand trust.

Value Proposition: A clear statement that explains what makes a product or service unique and why it is valuable to the customer.

Viral Marketing: A marketing technique that leverages social sharing to rapidly spread brand messages, often without a large budget.

Virtual Reality (VR) Marketing: The use of fully immersive digital environments to create engaging and experiential advertising campaigns, that is often used by automotive, real estate, and tourism industries.

Visual Branding: The use of design elements such as logos, color schemes, and typography to create a distinctive brand image.

Visual Hierarchy: The arrangement of elements in an ad that guides the viewer's eye toward the most important information, such as headlines, product images, and CTAs.

Voice Search Optimization (VSO): The process of optimizing content to rank for voice-based searches on smart assistants like Alexa, Siri, and Google Assistant.

References

1. Batista, E. (2011, July 31). *Antonio Damasio on Emotion and Reason*. Ed Batista. https://www.edbatista.com/2011/07/antonio-damasio-on-emotion-and-reason.html

2. BBC & Kannan, S. (2014, November 19). *How McDonald's conquered India*. BBC News. Retrieved January 6, 2025, from https://www.bbc.com/news/business-30115555

3. BBC News. (2013, September 11). *Google faces Streetview wi-fi snooping action*. BBC News. Retrieved January 15, 2025, from https://www.bbc.com/news/technology-24047235

4. The Brand Hopper. (2024, September 28). *A case study on Nike's "Dream Crazy" campaign*. The Brand Hopper. Retrieved November 15, 2024, from https://thebrandhopper.com/2024/09/28/a-case-study-on-nikes-dream-crazy-campaign/

5. Choice Hacking & Clinehens, J. (2022, March 7). *Apple's marketing case study: How the iPhone sells itself*. Choice Hacking. Retrieved November 15, 2024, from https://www.choicehacking.com/2022/03/07/apples-marketing-case-study-iphone/

6. Columbia Journalism Review & Gotfredson, S. G. (2024, December 12). *Spotify's Bad Wrap*. Columbia Journalism Review. Retrieved February 13, 2025, from https://www.cjr.org/the_media_today/spotify_wrapped_google_ai_podcast_journalism.php?

7. Forbes & Di Placido, D. (2024, December 5). *Spotify Wrapped 2024: Backlash, Controversy And Memes*. Forbes. Retrieved February 13, 2025, from https://www.forbes.com/sites/danidiplacido/2024/12/05/spotify-wrapped-2024-backlash-controversy-and-memes/

8. Kozlowska, I. (2018, April 300). *Facebook and Data Privacy in the Age of Cambridge Analytica*. The Henry M. Jackson School of International Studies. Retrieved January 15, 2025, from https://jsis.washington.edu/news/facebook-data-privacy-age-cambridge-analytica/

9. Mashed & Beach, H. (2022, January 26). *The Hilarious Translation Mistake KFC China Made With Its Slogan*. Mashed. Retrieved January 6, 2025, from https://www.mashed.com/747566/the-hilarious-translation-mistake-kfc-china-made-with-its-slogan/

10. The New York Times & Tsang, A. (2017, April 4). *Nivea Pulls 'White Is Purity' Ad After Online Uproar*. The New York Times. Retrieved January 6, 2025, from https://www.nytimes.com/2017/04/04/business/media/nivea-ad-online-uproar-racism.html

11. NPR & Xu, Y. (2018, December 1). *Dolce & Gabbana Ad (With Chopsticks) Provokes Public Outrage in China*. NPR. Retrieved January 5, 2025, from https://www.npr.org/sections/goatsandsoda/2018/12/01/671891818/dolce-gabbana-ad-with-chopsticks-provokes-public-outrage-in-china

12. Reuters & Singh, J. (2025, February 7). *Pinterest shares jump as AI advertisement tools drive forecasts*. Reuters. Retrieved February 8, 2025, from https://www.reuters.com/technology/pinterest-shares-jump-ai-advertisement-tools-drive-forecasts-2025-02-07/

13. 1Rival IQ & McCall, K. (2022, February 12). *Wendy's social media strategy: Lessons in brand voice and engagement*. Rival IQ. Retrieved November 16, 2024, from https://www.rivaliq.com/blog/wendys-social-media-strategy/

14. Roll, M. (2021, February n.d.). *The secret to Starbucks' brand success*. Martin Roll. Retrieved January 3, 2025, from https://martinroll.com/resources/articles/strategy/secret-starbucks-brand-success/

15. Smith Brothers Media. (2021, December 13). *Case study: Old Spice – Smell like a man, man*. Smith Brothers Media. Retrieved December 28, 2024, from https://smithbrothersmedia.com.au/get-smarter/case-study-old-spice-smell-like-a-man-man/

16. Tubular Labs & Worthen, H. (2022, February 28). *Airbnb's user-generated campaign & the post-COVID traveler*. Tubular Labs. Retrieved December 28, 2024, from https://tubularlabs.com/blog/airbnbs-user-generated-campaign-the-post-covid-traveler/

17. The Wall Street Journal & Graham, M. (2024, November 15). *Taco Bell and KFC's Owner Says AI-Driven Marketing Is Boosting Purchases*. The Wall Street Journal. Retrieved January 21, 2025, from https://www.wsj.com/articles/taco-bell-and-kfcs-owner-says-ai-driven-marketing-is-boosting-purchases-ab3a5f36

Reference Books

- **Influence: The Psychology of Persuasion** by Robert B. Cialdini (2021)
- **This Is Marketing** by Seth Godin (2018)
- **The New Rules of Marketing and PR** by David Meerman Scott (2020)
- **Hooked: How to Build Habit-Forming Products** by Nir Eyal (2014)
- **Generative AI-Driven Storytelling: A New Era for Marketing** by Marko Vidrih & Shiva Mayahi (2023)

NOTES

www.ingramcontent.com/pod-product-compliance
Lightning Source LLC
Chambersburg PA
CBHW050338270326
41926CB00016B/3507